# emotionalintelligenceworkbook

# emotionalintelligenceworkbook

The all-in-one guide for optimal personal growth!

Dr Ronél le Roux
Dr Rina de Klerk

Human & Rousseau
Cape Town   Pretoria

Dedicated to my husband, Carl, my children, Leon and Anika, and my parents. I appreciate
everyone's support and encouragement.

Thank you, Lord, for your love and mercy.

Rina, thanks for being there for me!

*Ronél*

Above all, my gratitude to my heavenly Father for so many blessings.

Thank you, Ronél, you are a special friend and colleague.

Dedicated to my husband, Hennie, my children, Jacques, Melandi, Michiel and Riko, and my parents.

Thank you very much for enhancing my emotional intelligence!

A special thank you to everyone who crossed my path and touched my life.

*Rina*

It is important that you practise the new skills in order to gain the maximum benefit from the book, but it is recommended that you attend the course as well. During the course you will be guided to reach your full potential by the integration of your new skills and knowledge.

Courses are aimed at adults, parents, teachers, therapists, children and companies. Contact the authors for more information about workshops, training and therapeutical services:

Dr Ronél le Roux
P.O. Box 2698
The Reeds
0158
*ronellr@mweb.co.za*

Dr Rina de Klerk
*hdeklerk@iafrica.com*

**In South Africa this book is only for the use of individuals and professionals in a one-to-one therapeutic situation. The contents may under no circumstances be used for groups in training situations, for courses, etc.**

First impression 2001
Second impression 2003
Third impression 2004
Fourth impression 2006

Copyright © 2001 by J.P. le Roux and H.J. de Klerk
Published by Human & Rousseau a division of NB Publishers (Pty) Limited,
40 Heerengracht, Cape Town
Typography by Susan Bloemhof
Cover design by Anna-Marie Petzer
Cover photograph: Image Bank
Illustrations by Colin Daniel (colindaniel@hotmail.com)
Illustrations on pp. 103 and 104 from *Brain gym® for all* (copyright © by Melodie de Jager)
Text electronically prepared and set in 11 on 13 pt Janson Text by ALINEA STUDIO, Cape Town
Printed and bound by Paarl Print, Oosterland Street, Paarl, South Africa

ISBN-10: 0-7981-4155-7
ISBN-13: 978-0-7981-4155-0

# TABLE OF CONTENTS

# GENERAL INTRODUCTION

A number of people claim that they were the first to formulate the term "emotional intelligence". However, it appears that Dr Claude Steiner was the first to define the term "emotional literacy" some years ago, and later Peter Salovey of Yale University and John Mayer of the University of New Hampshire formulated the term "emotional intelligence". They wrote several professional articles about the subject.

The importance of "emotional intelligence" (EI) came to light when Howard Gardner identified a spectrum of "intelligences" in his book *Frames of the mind* (1983). These intelligences are as follows: linguistic (language skills), logical-mathematical, musical (e.g. composers), bodily-kinaesthetic (e.g. athletes, surgeons), naturalistic and personal intelligence. Personal intelligence is divided in intra- and interpersonal intelligence, which includes *inter alia* the following: to experience and admit your feelings, to be able to control them, to motivate yourself (intra-) and to establish and maintain social relationships (inter-). Personal intelligence includes emotional intelligence. EI can be learnt and improved at any age by acquiring the skills and applying them to social situations. This cannot be done for most of the other intelligences. By improving your emotional intelligence you can reach your full potential; in other words, EI may help you to use you brain (intellect) more effectively.

Tests to determine emotional intelligence are being formulated worldwide, but the only real test for EI is life itself. *How do you cope with what is happening to you?*

There are two fairly common groups of people: (1) those who are not aware of their feelings and who cannot express them (often men) and (2) those who experience their feelings intensely and frequently express them inappropriately (women). The first group has to learn which feelings they are experiencing and how to express them. The second group has to learn how to control their feelings and to express them appropriately. People who are not emotionally proficient are not in touch with their feelings, and/or cannot control and express them. Poor communication and conflict resolution skills, low self-confidence and low self-acceptance often accompany this. These people may experience problems in establishing and maintaining relationships. They may have few goals and little motivation to do anything about it. This may give rise to alcoholism, drug abuse, eating problems (e.g. anorexia and bulimia), marital problems, depression and other difficulties.

## What is the purpose of this workbook?

This book has not been written to be read through passively and then put aside. In buying the book, you have committed yourself to experience it actively and to do all the activities. You need to apply your new knowledge and skills in social situations. With the help of this book, you can get to know yourself thoroughly.

The purpose of the book is not to give final definitions on EI. We will not try to explain emotions in terms of genetics or social origins, or try to show where precisely in the brain emotions are experienced. There will not be any explanations of the chemical processes that are associated with emotions. Instead, this is aimed at making the fundamental principles of EI part of your life by giving you both theory and practice. For the purposes of this book, we have concentrated only on the basic principles so as to make them worthwhile for each person. No aspects of it have been described in full.

This workbook is a direct and effective way to get in touch with your feelings and to establish loving relationships with others. When we are emotionally effective, we are able to cope with most difficult emotional situations. Emotional pain has to be expressed or else you lose contact with your feelings and you cannot understand or control them. You will be taught how to reach out to other people with your feelings and how to be empowered by love and not fear. It will be easier for you to understand and channel your own feelings, as well as listening to others and reacting to their needs. You will be able to repair emotional damage and to eliminate misunderstandings. You will reach into the world of feelings, situations, thoughts, etc.

## What is emotional intelligence?

Emotional intelligence is a type of personal and social intelligence, which includes the following:
* The ability to perceive, recognise, understand and react to the feelings of yourself and those of others (emotional awareness);
* The ability to distinguish between various feelings and to name them (emotional literacy);
* The ability to express and control your feelings appropriately (emotional control);
* The ability to listen to others, to have empathy with them and to communicate effectively in terms of emotions and thoughts, and
* To use the information in directing your thoughts and actions so that you live effectively, are motivated and have a goal in mind (relation between thoughts, feelings and behaviour).

## What are the benefits of being emotionally intelligent?

There are several benefits of being emotionally intelligent:
* You gain emotional awareness that enables you to recognise your own feelings. You know the difference between feelings and behaviour and what their origin is.
* It is possible for you to find a balance between expressing and controlling your feelings.
* There is a balance between your thoughts and feelings.
* You realise that you are responsible for your own feelings.
* You have empathy with the feelings of others and can understand them.
* Your improved communication skills give rise to healthier relationships with others.
* You have the skills to assert yourself. You provide for fulfilling your needs without intruding into the rights of others.
* It is possible for you to formulate goals that make your life interesting and make you more effective.

* Emotional baggage can be left behind while your increasing energy makes it possible for the "new you" to strive towards new ideals.

## How to make the best of the workbook

Keep the following in mind while working through the book:
* Firstly, always work through the theoretical part where information about each new skill or section is given. Make sure that you understand what it is all about and how it applies to your situation. It is important not to skip certain parts as these parts follow one another and form a whole. Important information and insights can be lost if sections are omitted.
* It is important to do each activity as fully as possible, even if you think that you have mastered the skill already or that it is not applicable to your situation. Possible answers to certain activities (marked with a *) are given at the back of the book.
* Don't be in a hurry to work through the book. When you have done a section, take time to reflect, think about it, apply what you have learnt in social situations and practise the new skills.
* After working through the book, go back and study it again. Information of this kind has to be studied again and again before it can be integrated. The new knowledge has to become part of you; in other words you have to know it very well.
* People differ in their level of EI. Take what you have to work on most, e.g. recognition of feelings, and concentrate more on that than on the other parts.
* Remember that people learn in different ways, e.g. by seeing, hearing, experiencing, etc. Depending on your particular learning style, you might have to focus more on the integration of the theory or experiencing the activities. It may be a combination of both. Your learning style can be determined professionally.[1]
* This book is not a quick fix that will suddenly remedy everything in yourself and your relationships. It depends on you whether you work on those things that have to change. You have to consciously decide to change. **Be assured that this book will make a difference to your life!**
* Don't believe everything in the book unconditionally – there are so many different ways of thinking and confirmed truths that contradict one another that one must remain critical. Think about the

book in depth, question it and then come to your own conclusions (truth). An important goal of this book is to get you to think about yourself and that which you believe in. There is no such thing as an absolute right or wrong. What is important is how you think and feel, and what works for you in certain circumstances.

• Not everything you do/think/feel at the moment needs to be changed. Frequently you get confirmation that what you are currently doing is correct and that you have to keep it up.

Remember that the changing process often brings about resistance because it is more comfortable staying unchanged. Furthermore, it is important to remember that you can only change in yourself if you consciously decide to change. Nobody can do it for you. You cannot change another person. You can change your own behaviour and your reaction to the behaviour of another person. (How do you react to the feelings and behaviour of others?) Risk to be different and better. New behaviour has to be practised

regularly before it comes naturally. Don't wait until you feel ready/comfortable about the new knowledge before you start practising it. Start immediately to practise the new behaviour and to apply the newly gained knowledge. You will feel comfortable about it as soon as you see the results.

Read the following statement carefully and then apply it to yourself:

"If you always do what you've always done, you always get what you've always got. So if you want something different, do something different."
*Anonymous*

In the first three chapters we will focus on intrapersonal skills and in the following chapters on interpersonal skills.

**Are you ready to start the changing process? Are you prepared to let go of old habits, behaviour and thinking patterns and to learn new ones? If you are ready, let us begin . . .**

# CHAPTER 1
## Becoming emotionally aware

The first part of the book focuses on your awareness of your inner self and that which happens in other people as well. This awareness is a prerequisite for any change which you want to make in yourself and it is the basis of social relationships. How can we start a relationship with someone and maintain it without knowing what we and the other person feel and experience?

In order to gain more clarity about your own emotional awareness, answer the following questionnaire.[2] Please answer these questions as honestly as possible. If you cannot decide whether your answer is Yes or No, answer Not Sure.

## ACTIVITY 1: Emotional awareness questionnaire

| No. | Question | YES | NO | NOT SURE |
|---|---|---|---|---|
| 1A | I have noticed that sometimes when I find myself with a person who is very emotional I am surprisingly calm and without feeling. | ✓ | | |
| 1B | At times when I am about to interact with people I don't know well, I feel sensations like heart palpitations, stomach cramps, a lump or dryness in the throat, or shortness of breath, but I don't know why this is happening. | ✓ | | |
| 1C | Sometimes I am flooded by emotions that disorganise and confuse me. | ✓ | | |
| 1D | From time to time, I am aware of having feelings of anger, from slight irritation to rage. | ✓ | | |
| 1E | If another person is emotional, I am usually able to tell what emotion they are feeling, such as fear, happiness, sadness, hope or anger. | ✓ | | |
| 1F | I enjoy situations in which people are having strong positive emotions of love, hope and joy, like at weddings or church services. | | ✓ | |
| 2A | Sometimes after a difficult time with another person, I feel as if parts of my body are numb. | | ✓ | |
| 2B | I take one or more over-the-counter drugs to deal with headaches, stomach and digestive problems, or bodily pains that my doctor cannot explain. | | ✓ | |

| No. | Question | YES | NO | NOT SURE |
|-----|----------|-----|-----|----------|
| 2C | I know I have very strong feelings, but I am frequently unable to discuss them with other people. | ✓ | | |
| 2D | I am aware of having feelings of fear, ranging from apprehension to terror. | ✓ | | |
| 2E | Sometimes I can feel other people's feelings in my body. | | ✓ | |
| 2F | Other people appreciate me because I know how to cool down emotional situations. | ✓ | | |
| 3A | I can easily kill a small animal like a snake or chicken without feeling anything in particular. | | ✓ | |
| 3B | I am often jumpy and irritable, and I can't help it. | ✓ | | |
| 3C | I find myself lying about feelings because I am embarrassed to speak about them. | ✓ | | |
| 3D | I am aware of having strong feelings of love and joy. | | ✓ | |
| 3E | I often do things for other people because I sympathise with them and then can't say "no". | ✓ | | |
| 3F | I am good at helping people sort out their emotions because I usually understand why they are feeling them. | ✓ | | |
| 4A | I can be around people who are suffering physical pain without getting upset about it. | | ✓ | |
| 4B | I get sweaty palms when I'm with people I don't know. | | | ✓ |
| 4C | I know I have strong feelings, but most of the time I don't know what those feelings are. | ✓ | | |
| 4D | I am pretty good at knowing what I feel and why. | | ✓ | |
| 4E | Sometimes other people's feelings are very clear to me and that can be a problem. | | ✓ | |
| 4F | I can usually handle people who have strong feelings and unload them on me. | | ✓ | |
| 5A | I am almost always a rational person and have no problems with my emotions. | | ✓ | |
| 5B | I have been in love and suddenly, inexplicably lost that feeling completely. | | ✓ | |

| No. | QUESTION | YES | NO | NOT SURE |
|-----|----------|-----|-----|----------|
| 5C | I am overwhelmed by bad moods sometimes. | ✓ | | |
| 5D | When I have to make an important decision, I usually know how I feel about it, whether to be scared, excited, angry, or some other combination of emotions. | | ✓ | |
| 5E | In a competitive situation in which I am winning or clearly superior, I feel sorry for the other person. | | ✓ | |
| 5F | When I am in a room full of people, I can tell how the group is feeling – excited, angry, bored or scared. | ✓ | | |
| 6A | I very, very rarely cry. | ✓ | | |
| 6B | Sometimes when I watch a TV commercial, tears come to my eyes, and I don't really understand why. | | ✓ | |
| 6C | Sometimes when I am feeling bad, I can't tell if I am scared or angry. | | ✓ | ✓ |
| 6D | I am a person who sometimes feels shame and guilt. | ✓ | | |
| 6E | If I had the opportunity to shoot an animal like a bird, rabbit or deer I would not be able to do it because I would feel sorry for the animal. | ✓ | | |
| 6F | I often change the way I act towards another person because I feel it will make things easier between us. | ✓ | | |

## RESULTS OF EMOTIONAL AWARENESS QUESTIONNAIRE (ACTIVITY 1)

Count the number of "Yes" answers you have given for all the "A" questions, then the "Yes" answers for "B", etc. until you have a number (1-6) for each letter. Count only the "Yes" answers. Record your scores here:

A ...2...

B ...2...

C ...5...

D ...2...

E ...3...

F ...4...

Mark the columns below according to the scores which you allocated to yourself above, e.g. if you attained five for C, make an X in each of the first five blocks (from 1 to 5).

| | A Numbness | B Symptoms | C Prim. exper. | D Differentiate | E Empathy | F Interactive |
|---|---|---|---|---|---|---|
| 6 | | | | | | |
| 5 | | | X | | | |
| 4 | | | X | | | X |
| 3 | | | X | | X | X |
| 2 | X | X | X | X | X | X |
| 1 | X | X | X | X | X | X |

## INTERPRETING YOUR SCORE ON THE "EMOTIONAL AWARENESS QUESTIONNAIRE"

The goal is to strive towards a high emotional awareness profile.

This is a short explanation of the different categories:

**A. Numbness:** People who score a high number in this category are numb regarding feelings and can be described as cold/blunt. They are unaware that feelings can physically be felt in their bodies. This is possibly worse in certain situations. This person is frequently one who can stay calm in crisis situations and can lead the group.

**B. Physical symptoms/sensations:** These people experience the physical sensations of feelings, e.g. the contracting of muscles in their neck or stomach, but they do not realise that they are afraid or angry. They do not associate the physical symptoms with what they are experiencing, e.g. if the person experiences stress and has a headache as a result, he will take some medication. However, he will not do anything to relieve the stress. People in this category may use or abuse several kinds of medication in order to control the physical symptoms of their feelings.

**C. Primitive experience:** The person experiences feelings as heightened levels of energy, but he still

does not understand them and is unable to talk about them. This person is extremely vulnerable to emotions that he cannot control. It is possible that he may have uncontrolled emotional outbursts, be impulsive or depressed. This person is often the first to suffer a setback as a result of stress and it is essential for him to become emotionally more effective.

**Verbal barrier:** Crossing the linguistic barrier requires an environment that is friendly to emotional information. If there is no-one willing to listen to the person's feelings and needs, he will never learn to express them. Mutual expression of feelings is necessary to enhance emotional awareness.

**D. Differentiation:** The person is able to recognise different feelings and their intensity and can talk about them. He understands the difference between basic feelings and realises that he may experience different feelings in the same situation. He knows that an initial feeling can intensify, e.g. from angry to furious, and that one feeling can lead to another, e.g. first hurt and then anger.

**Causality (not indicated on the chart):** As he begins to understand the exact nature of his feelings, he also begins to understand the causes of those feelings, in other words the events that trigger his emotional responses. He understands that his behaviour can lead to certain feelings in other people.

**E. Empathy:** The person becomes intuitively aware of the different feelings which other people experience. This is learnt during childhood; some people are naturally empathetic, while others are totally unaware of the feelings of others. Empathy is frequently incorrect. You have to ask for confirmation, e.g. "Do you feel unhappy?" "No, I am very frustrated."

**F. Interactivity:** In order to reach this level, you have to know how people react to the feelings of others and whether the interaction will be positive or negative. It is the most sophisticated level of emotional awareness: to know what you and others feel and to be able to predict how emotions will influence each other. You can use your emotional awareness to have more comfortable, positive and constructive interactions with others.

## EMOTIONAL AWARENESS PROFILES
### Low awareness profile

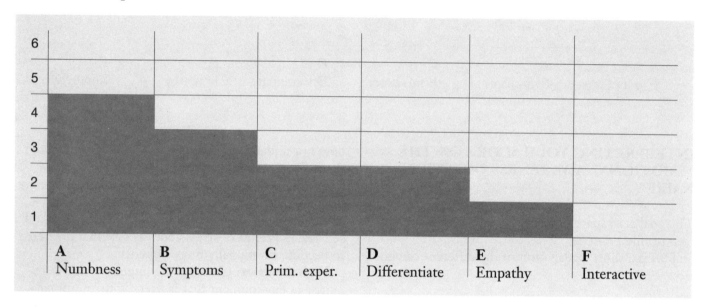

### Average awareness profile

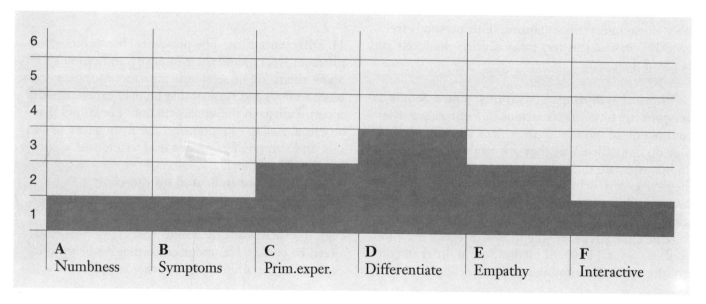

## High awareness profile

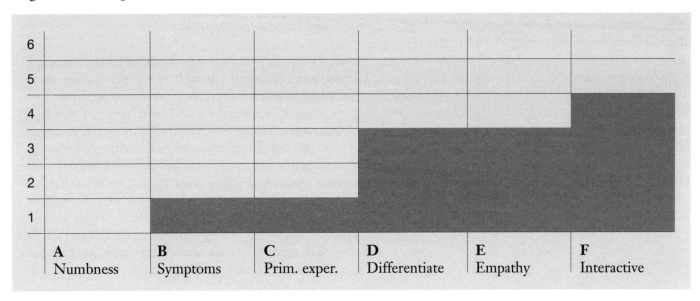

Your chart may not look like any of the above. A person can be numb in certain situations (especially with regard to himself), but at the same time be able to have empathy with others. The goal is to reach a high emotional awareness.

Now that you know more about your own awareness, we can take a look at what feelings actually are and where they originate. Remember that the mere enhancement of your emotional awareness may give rise to your experiencing your emotions more intensely, but you will not necessarily function better as a result. There are several skills that have to be developed before you will notice an improvement in yourself. It may at first be difficult for you to see the relations between the different aspects, but you will soon get the full picture.

## FEELINGS

When we think about feelings, we tend to think only about a basic few. Some writers believe that there are just a few basic feelings like sadness, anger, expectation, pleasure, acceptance, fear, surprise and disgust. They allege that all other feelings are just combinations of these. Other writers only distinguish between pleasure and pain in terms of the past, present and future. What is important here is to realise that there are many more feelings than we realise. Mostly we are not aware of the origin of our feelings or what we should do about them. In the following section your knowledge about feelings will quickly be improved!

### What is a feeling?

A feeling is an internal physical reaction to something you experience (a stimulus). A stimulus can be something you perceive through your senses and about which you make an interpretation or it can be a certain thought you have. Feelings are always internal. We use noticeable behaviour to communicate our feelings, e.g. crying or laughing. All emotions are forms of energy and can provide energy. Feelings of love and anger can both generate energy to allow you to behave in a certain way. Feelings are characteristic of the human race and are a natural and wonderful part of yourself. They are one trait all people have and which gives us a sense of community. Feelings are both consciously and unconsciously generated. The environment (socialisation) and the genetic composition of a person both play a role in the origin of feelings.

The better you understand your own feelings, the better you can understand those of others. Remember that you cannot enjoy feelings if you are unaware of them. (How can you enjoy feelings of happiness if you are not aware of them?) You cannot express feelings if you suppress or ignore them.

Research shows that a couple of chemical processes take place in your body when you experience feelings.[3] This indicates to us that emotions do not only "happen" in our head, but the whole body is influenced and involved. The fact that continuous anxiety can lower our immunity can thus be explained.

**What happens when we do not experience and accept our feelings (suppress them)?**
1. Feelings that are not experienced and accepted may lead to physical illness and symptoms such as stomach pains, migraine, back pain, stiff neck, ulcers, regular colds, asthma and insomnia.

2. They can give rise to compulsive behaviour, e.g. smoking, drinking, use of drugs, overworking, overeating, too much exercising, obsessive meditation, continuous socialisation and other types of obsessive behaviour. Determine what is causing your compulsive behaviour and evaluate your feelings after each compulsive stage. Do you feel better afterwards? It is only by accepting and experiencing feelings that you can get rid of compulsive behaviour that can negatively influence your quality of life.

3. You may say and do the wrong things at the wrong times or don't say and do anything.

4. You can cut off feelings and intellectualise, rationalise (think about excuses) or lose contact with reality.

To accept your feelings, you have to be aware of them and accept them as your own.

Don't let the experiencing of strong feelings frighten you. If you don't fully accept them, you will never learn what they are, where they come from and what the cause was. You may blame yourself and others, or feel sad about feelings you do not accept. People who are unable to accept their own feelings blame others for their anger, or they convince themselves that their feelings of sadness and anxiety are something to be ashamed of. Difficult feelings that are only experienced in part are distorted. This wastes time and energy and blurs your senses.

Acceptance of your feelings shows you that you are able to cope with any feeling irrespective of its intensity. Remember that humour and laughter are worthy tools in the acceptance of feelings. Acceptance makes it easier to laugh at your mistakes. **To laugh brings you into your body** – it is like exercise for the inner you.

You have to be able to experience, accept and enjoy positive feelings. Are you able to experience and enjoy feelings of excitement, sensuality and love for more than just a few minutes? Let yourself enjoy the pleasant feeling and let it intensify by deep breathing and experiencing it in full in your body. The reward for emotional acceptance is more intense positive feelings that last longer and more intense unpleasant feelings that are quickly something of the past.

**Note:** For the purpose of this book we do not distinguish between emotions and feelings, and they are treated as synonyms.

## Why are feelings important?

Each emotion is "a wake-up call" to tell you that you have to give attention to something important. We do differentiate between positive and negative feelings, but it is important to remember that a negative or less pleasant emotion is valuable because it indicates an unmet need. It is therefore essential that you do not suppress "negative" emotions.

Feelings ought to motivate you, to make you ask questions and to act in order to change something. Goleman[4] pointed out that the word "emotion" is derived from the Latin word "motere" which implies movement. The more passion you have about something, the more motivated you are to do something about it. It is usually the strongest emotions that spur you on. How many good performances are frequently the result of frustration? Remember that people have different levels of emotional energy, which is reflected by their personalities (cautious/relaxed, spontaneous/withdrawn) and the slow or quick way in which they do their daily tasks. You will have to react to them differently. These energy levels can be measured.[5]

Feelings are contagious. One depressed person in a family or working environment can influence the others negatively. The more energetic you are, the more you are able to withstand this "contagiousness".

You have to strive for balance between your feelings and your reason. We do not want to imply that the one is more important than the other – they should be in balance.

Remember that feelings are signals for your body to determine what is right and what your needs are. Sometimes you can experience a feeling erroneously, as a result of your interpretation or your automatic patterns (the behaviour you do not think about). It is your responsibility to verify what the reality is. If you are used to driving in South Africa (automatic pattern) and suddenly you have to drive in the USA on the "wrong" side of the road, it will feel uncomfortable and wrong, although you will cognitively know that you are doing it right. The feeling is therefore not justified. Feelings motivate us to examine the past, to fill the present and to find a different path in the future.

"You can handle people more successfully by enlisting their feelings than by convincing their reason."
*Anonymous*

## The origin of a feeling

The information you gather through your senses (sight, hearing, smell, taste and touch) is interpreted in terms of your values, assumptions, previous experiences, etc. This happens very quickly and automatically; in about the time you take to snap your fingers. Although this process is not always conscious, you do have a choice about how you interpret this information. We can thus decide from which point of view we want to look at certain information.

We give control away to others when we think that other people are causing our feelings, e.g. when you say "you are making me angry" or when you think that it is because you do not have a job that you are depressed. We are dependent on other people in order to experience positive feelings and their behaviour can easily cause negative feelings within us.

If you have always seen people who have lots of self-confidence as full of themselves and irritating, you can change the way you look at them by starting to think about them as people who worked hard to be where they are. On the other hand, you may admire them, which will give rise to more positive feelings. The way you interpret (think about) the information you receive determines to a large extent your feelings about it. We can control our feelings by controlling our interpretation of the information and also our reaction or noticeable behaviour which is a result of the interpretation. Your behaviour will not be impulsive because you have thought about it logically. If you do not think before you react, your behaviour could be very impulsive and you could do something which you later regret. Remember that you have a choice about how you want to behave.

**Stimulus → Think about it, decide → Your behaviour (Interpret)**

**The origin of a feeling can be seen as follows:**

1. He whispers something. (Stimulus.)

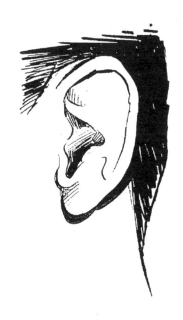

2. Senses pick up the information.

3. Interpretation takes place according to your assumptions/beliefs. Did they talk about me? What did they say and why? Your interpretation may be negative or positive – it determines your feelings and behaviour.

4. Negative: Discouraged – what did they say about me?

5. Positive: It was not about me! (feeling and behaviour)

### What do you feel?

Children are very honest in the expression of their feelings. There is a tendency to suppress or deny your feelings as you get older in such a way that you might lose the ability to identify or experience your feelings. It is very important that you are aware of your body – are you comfortable or uncomfortable? Cold or warm? Are you hungry or satisfied? You have to experience your feelings physically to determine whether they are pleasant or unpleasant. Where in your body do you experience, for example, anger? Fear is usually associated with a stiffening or contraction in various body parts, while anger is experienced as heat or excessive energy in your stomach, chest or throat. Sadness can be described as a pain in your chest or a heavy feeling in your whole body, pleasure is an uplifting, relieving sensation, while love is felt in the vicinity of the heart.

It is easier to recognise your feelings if your body is fit. Exercise and movement are important – especially to music. Walking is very good for you. Develop and use all of your senses. Are you capable of perceiving and distinguishing between various sounds, odours and visual information? Remember that it is through our senses that we discover and experience the world around us. Ensure that you know the difference between the information you gain from your senses and the interpretations you make as a result. These two often differ to a large extent. Practise the recognition of different feelings by visualising situations where you were afraid, jealous or angry. Try to recognise the different emotions in your body. You have to be able to focus on intense feelings without getting anxious or fearful.

Repressed feelings demand a lot of energy. Practise the acceptance of feelings by saying to yourself: **"I may feel angry, I may feel upset, I may feel sad."** You will find that the intensity of the feeling will diminish. **Emotion and behaviour are not equal to each other, which implies that all feelings are acceptable but not all behaviour is.** The way in which you cope with the feeling or react to it may thus be destructive.

If you give the correct name to the feeling, you will feel more energetic; the intensity of the feeling will diminish and you will realise that you are correct in your recognition of the specific feeling. Your brain knows that it is possible that you will cope more effectively with the feeling if you named it correctly. The ability to put words to your feelings, to understand the words, to choose the appropriate reaction to the feeling from all the possible internal responses, is a sign of high self-awareness and emotional intelligence.

Specific physical symptoms may later be associated with a specific feeling. If you can become aware of the physical symptoms as soon as they arise, you may be able to predict which feeling you will experience. You can think about it and make the correct decision or act appropriately. You get the opportunity to think logically and you gain a balance between your feelings and your reason. Do you often react in a specific way when you experience a specific feeling? How do you react to a feeling of embarrassment or when you are feeling stressed? Use your powers of reasoning – what is the best (constructive) reaction to the feeling you experience?

Emotional awareness helps you to distinguish between a variety of simultaneous feelings. We usually react or speak as a result of the strongest feeling, but it is not always appropriate as you may insult someone when you are upset. Try to discriminate between the feelings, and decide which feeling you want to react to.

Keep a strong emotional attachment to your needs and values so that you may defend what feels right to you. If a decision feels right to you, it is frequently correct, as long as you do not harm others or ignore their rights. You do not always need to justify your decisions. When you feel torn between external demands, become quiet and focus on your feelings. If you give attention to what your feelings tell you, you will have the energy to give attention to other things as well.

Your brain sends signals to your body to prepare it for "fight or flight" when you are afraid, or think that something is amiss. Frequently you experience the changes in your body and only then realise that you have had a fright, are stressed or afraid. It is important that you determine the origin of your feelings in order to do something about them.

**This is what happens in your body when you experience stress.** (It is not good for your body to be in a constant state of heightened stress.)

**Pupils dilate.**

**Heart beats faster.**

**You take quicker breaths.**

**Hollow feeling in stomach develops.**

**Hands are cold or sweaty.**

**Muscles contract.**

**Feet are cold.**

See if you can associate the feelings and physical symptoms in the following activity.

## ACTIVITY 2: Physical symptoms of feelings

Write the number of the feeling next to the symptoms associated with it as you experience them in your body. Different feelings may have the same symptoms.

1. Anger

2. Depression

3. Happiness

4. Fear

5. Worry

6. Sadness

7. Excitement

1/4/7 Heart beats faster
2/5/6 Continuously wants to sleep
1/4/5 Chest tightens
......... Feeling nauseous 4/5/2
1/4/5/7 Fast and shallow breathing
......... Feeling light and energetic 3
4 ......... Tired/arms paralysed
2/4/5/6 Heavy, dark feeling in the heart
......... Hands sweating 4/7/5
4/5/2 Muscles stiff/painful neck, shoulders
......... Cold and shaky 4/5
1/4 ......... Headaches
......... Warm/comfortable 3/7
4/1 ..... Muscles contract
......... Lump in the throat 4/6

# ACTIVITY 3: Experience a feeling in your body

Start this activity by doing the following. Sit like someone who feels very dispirited – shoulders hanging, head hanging, eyes downcast. Then sit erect, eyes lifted, shoulders back and say aloud to yourself: "Yes!" Do it as if you have just won a big prize. Can you feel the difference in your energy levels?

Use the following process as a guideline to practise experiencing a feeling in your body (visualise it or become aware of it while you experience the feeling). Start with less intense feelings – they may be positive, pleasant feelings as well. Don't go to sleep after the exercise. Wash the dishes or read something, since your brain cannot distinguish between imagination and reality. You have to complete the visualised feeling before you resume your daily tasks.

1. Prepare a peaceful, comfortable place where you can seclude yourself for a few minutes.
2. Try not to think about anything and breathe deeply. Close your eyes.
3. Relax your body.
4. Take your time to explore your whole body, perceive the various physical and emotional sensations and determine where in your body the most intense emotion is situated. If you can only recognise a cold/numb feeling, concentrate on that feeling.
5. Let the feeling intensify by deep breathing. Try to imagine the air going to where the emotion is. Remain aware of the feeling (experience it) and attempt not to think about it.
6. Focus like this for 5 to 10 minutes, increase it to 20 minutes or do it for 2 or 3 minutes. If you can, do it 2 or 3 times a day.
7. End the exercise by taking your attention away from your emotions and physical feelings and start with your daily responsibilities.

If you are unable to experience a feeling, visualise a situation in which you had some strong feelings. Wait until you are used to the process before you try this with very strong feelings. As soon as you experience the feelings, focus only on them and stop thinking about the reasons for them. Be patient with the process – it can take 2 to 3 months to fully master it.

The following exercise may help you to tolerate and accept intense feelings which you are experiencing at that moment or which you have experienced in the past (emotional memories). Remember that energy is absorbed by difficult feelings that come to the fore continuously. You will have more energy for other activities if you can accept these feelings.

Before you start the exercise, go for a walk, dance or do some exercises to music. End the exercise with this as well.

The exercise:
1. Relax, don't think about anything and breathe deeply.
2. Become aware of the most intense feeling in your body (as was done in the previous exercise). Breathe deeply and let it intensify.
3. Ask yourself the following questions, but stay focused on the feeling and not on the thoughts about it.

**Questions:**
Are you a new feeling?

_____
_____
_____

If not, how old are you? When did I experience you for the first time?

_____

_____

_____

Do I experience you often or just now and then?

_____

_____

_____

What kind of feeling is it?

_____

_____

_____

Is it sadness or hurt? If it is sadness, why do I feel sad?

_____

_____

_____

Is it anger or frustration? Why?

_____

_____

_____

Is it fear? Why?

_____

_____

_____

Is it joy, happiness or enthusiasm? Why?

_____

_____

_____

If you do not get any answers, accept it but keep doing the exercise.[6]

**Discriminate between old and new feelings:** Transferring old feelings to new situations is a mistake everyone makes some time in his/her life. It happens when you have not processed a previous situation/feeling and a new similar or different situation arises which brings with it all the feelings of the past situation. You may get very upset and react inappropriately. An example of this is as follows: A person did not go through the grieving process after a loved one died. After a while he loses a beloved pet and suddenly he experiences overwhelming feelings of loss and grief, which are possibly not totally applicable to the new situation. Another example of this is when you are cross with your husband but you argue with your children. Feelings are carried over from one situation to another even when the situations are not similar. Evaluate the situation in which you are and be aware of the transference of old feelings to the new situation. A person will experience appropriate feelings in a situation when he usually takes care to accept and process the feelings which accompany his experiences. The more you recognise and process your feelings, the less you will transfer old feelings inappropriately to new situations.

## ACTIVITY 4: Old feeling – new situation

Write down a situation where you transferred an old feeling to a new situation and how you behaved inappropriately as a result of that.

Old feeling:

_____
_____
_____
_____
_____
_____

The new situation:

_____
_____
_____
_____
_____
_____
_____

Your behaviour:

_____
_____
_____
_____
_____
_____

Consequences of your behaviour:

_____
_____
_____
_____
_____
_____

The following is a list of feeling words that will help you to enlarge your feeling vocabulary. We tried to distinguish between the feelings, but there may still be an overlap. Study these words to help you in your description of the feelings you experience.

## LIST OF FEELING WORDS

| **Happy** | **Sad** | **Angry** | **Afraid** | **Excited** |
|---|---|---|---|---|
| Excited | Tired | Furious | Confused | Alert |
| Boisterous | Hurt | Murderous | Unthankful | Concerned |
| Interested | Anxious | Inaccessible | Discontented | Elated |
| Mischievous | Frustrated | Insensitive | Inexperienced | Enthusiastic |
| Thankful | Guilty | Upset | Fearful | Involved |
| Pleased | Bewildered | Alarmed | Panicky | Stimulated |
| In love | Shocked | Embittered | Timid | Aroused |
| Believing | Cheated | Rebellious | Insecure | Busy |
| Naughty | Deceived | Aggressive | Tormented | Delighted |
| Cheerful | Hysterical | Jealous | Threatened | Elevated |
| Relaxed | Idiotic | Betrayed | Uneasy | Exhilarated |
| Happy | Apathetic | Bedevilled | Tense | Impatient |
| Relieved | Indifferent | Aggrieved | Appalled | Curious |
| Peaceful | Innocent | Irritated | Suspicious | Anxious |
| Friendly | Depressed | Belittled | Sceptical | Hyperactive |
| Confident | Burdened | Insulted | Guarded | Engaged |
| Patient | Lonely | Intolerant | Horrified | Intrigued |
| Invigorated | Desolate | Outcast | Stunned | Thrilled |
| Blissful | Withdrawn | Neglected | Anxious | Attentive |
| Carefree | Pensive | Moody | Reluctant | Energetic |
| Hearty | Inferior | Defensive | Impatient | Motivated |
| Equipped | Distressed | Vicious | Unsure | Optimistic |
| Refreshed | Miserable | Frustrated | Nervous | Alive |
| Safe | Awful | Provocative | Jittery | Jubilant |
| Wonderful | Sorry | Hate | Scared | Self-reliant |
| Calm | Cheerless | Resentful | Overwhelmed | Lively |
| Stable | Uncertain | Paranoiac | Intimidated | Adequate |
| Determined | Disappointed | Agonised | Desperate | Daring |
| Romantic | Embittered | Misused | Vulnerable | Determined |
| Agreeable | Perplexed | Trampled upon | Horrified | Assured |
| Ecstatic | Negative | Unsettled | Defensive | Potent |
| Energetic | Mournful | Abused | Apprehensive | Assertive |
| Loved | Jealous | Irresponsible | Swamped | Accomplished |
| Optimistic | Unmotivated | Cheated | Startled | Capable |
| Fulfilled | Incomplete | Despised | Awed | Bold |
| Joyful | Unloved | Provoked | Concerned | Dynamic |

## How do we identify a feeling?

Feelings may be identified in different ways, e.g. by looking at facial expressions; nonverbal signs like frowns, tight lips or by body posture that may be open or closed.

**Facial expressions** are valuable indications of feeling, especially with people on television, in restaurants and other social situations. Is the expression positive, negative or neutral? An open body posture is one that is relaxed and radiates warmth. A closed body posture is tense and cold, with the message: "Leave me alone, stay away." Emotionally intelligent people are able to read the **nonverbal messages** from others and react to them correctly. It is important to be sensitive to the moods of those around you, in order not to expect something from a person who does not feel up to it. Ask the person: "You look very sad. Are you?" The person then may answer: "No, actually I am ill." Your behaviour towards the person will depend on his answer. Remember that you can easily misunderstand a person's body language and feelings. It is therefore safer to ask for confirmation before you come to any mistaken conclusions. When you perceive a certain facial expression, look at the context in which it appears. The context may give you an indication whether your interpretation of the feeling from your frame of reference is correct or not.

**Music** is a strong communicator of emotion. What influence does music have on you? When do you listen to what kind of music? Listen with your whole body, calm yourself internally and became aware of your feelings. Remember though that not everybody can study with background music.

**Art**: Look at colour, form, shadow and texture. Visualise the art in the activity in different colours and see if it makes a difference in the feelings you are experiencing. Colours play an important role in our feelings. Buildings and places may stir certain feelings in you. It is your responsibility to evaluate the impact of your environment on you. Your office may cause a morbid mood but other colours can do wonders for you!

Your environment (e.g. buildings, places, television, stories, etc.) makes a continuous impact on your senses. See to it that you do not programme yourself with negative emotions! Remember that it is your responsibility to understand what impact these emotions have on your daily life and to make changes if necessary in order to have more positive feelings.

Do the following activity with regard to the identification of feelings: faces, nonverbal communication, art, stories and music. Where you have to identify feelings within yourself (art and music) try not to think about it. Just feel!

## ACTIVITY 5: Identify feelings*

Try to identify the different feelings that you perceive in people. Determine the intensity of the feeling as well. Remember that it is possible to experience two contrasting emotions at the same time, e.g. surprise and shock. One may smile, but feel sad. Where you can see the body or a large part of it, try to determine the feelings of the person by looking at his/her body language. Write down which feelings you experience when you look at a work of art. There are no right or wrong answers – each person will see/experience things differently.

| Faces | Nonverbal communication | Art | Stories | Music |
|---|---|---|---|---|
| 1. Pleasure & Suprise | 1. Shock | 1. Duality 1) is confronting the issue 2) is scared to confront | 1. Frustration Guilt Depression He feels inadequate | 1. |
| 2. Questioning / uncertanty | 2. slight embaressment – girl Pride – man | 2. I experience confusion – depression not positive | 2. Guilt Frustration unsure he is right in his action | 2. |
| 3. Sorrow/ despair | 3. Anger – a lot | 3. no feeling but like the 3D | 3. Acceptance Full of life Happiness self satisfaction | 3. |
| 4. Worry concern | 4. joy at recognition | 4. pleasure | 4. Doubt Fear Insecurity | 4. |
| 5. I experience confusion | 5. blissful self awareness | 5. dissatisfaction | | 5. |
| 6. Disapproval | 6. Need | 6. indecision | | |

**Faces**

1.

2.

3.

4.

5.

6.

## Nonverbal communication

1.

2.

3.

4.

5.

6.

**Art**

1.

2.
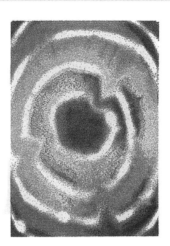

3.

4.

5.

6.
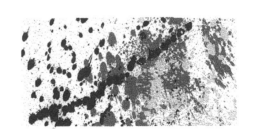

**Stories[7]**

1.
The story of a middle-aged man:
   Everything at work is falling behind. I have worked many late nights and as a result my wife and daughter think that I am neglecting them. My relationship with them is troubled. I feel I am neglecting them emotionally. I also feel guilty for not spending more time with them.
   In the meantime a close family member has moved in with us after his divorce and retrenchment from work. We are not enjoying any privacy and I have advised him to seek other lodgings. It was extremely difficult for me as I was brought up not to treat a guest like that.

Which of the following feelings are present in this man?
   What is the intensity of his feelings?

Depression
Frustration
Guilt
Energy
Happiness

Can you identify any other feelings?

2.
The story of a forty-year-old man:
I have written a letter to my ex-wife in which I explain that I cannot send her more money. She has just spent a huge amount on behalf of our daughter and expects me to recompense her. I cannot make her understand that I can't afford such a large expense. After I wrote the letter I energetically exercised in the gym and it really helped me to calm down and feel better.

Which of the following feelings occur?
   In what intensity do the feelings occur?

Composure
Happiness
Anxiety
Acceptance
Guilt
Frustration
Satisfaction

Can you identify any other feelings?

3.
Story of a middle-aged woman:
A few days ago it was my birthday. I have just spoken to a good friend of mine on the telephone. We discussed age, growing older and our dreams. She made me feel good because she reminded me of all the good things that are happening in my life and the fact that I am fulfilling some of my dreams. A couple of years ago things were more difficult and I made certain adaptations. After our chat I now realise that I have worked very hard to be where I am. I enjoy where I am now. I enjoy it a lot.

Which of the following emotions occur?
   In what intensity do they occur?

Jealousy
Full of life
Shame
Acceptance
Energetic
Happiness

Can you identify any other feelings?

4.
The story of a young girl:
I got a message that I had to phone him back. He apparently wants to arrange a lunch date with me. I can't gather enough courage to do it. Apparently he is intelligent and attractive! I know we might get along well, but I wonder whether he will like me. In the recent past my relationships with men have not worked out and I don't know why. Perhaps I should phone – it may work this time.

Which of the following emotions occur?
   In what intensity?

Hope
Doubt
Excitement
Inferiority
Happiness
Fear

Can you identify any other feelings?

**Music:**
Try to listen for about 20 seconds to the following music:

1. **Mozart:** "Allegro 1" from *Eine Kleine Nachtmusik*

2. **Syrinx (a South African group):** "Aranjuex" (from *Pan Flute Music*)

3. **Strauss, Johann II:** *Thunder and lightning polka*

4. **Neil Diamond:** *He ain't heavy, he's my brother* (The Greatest Collection, Vol. 2, RPM Records)

5. **Strauss, Johann II:** *Radetzsky march*

These pieces of music are only examples for you to listen to. If it is impossible for you to listen to them, listen to a variety of music. Listen and perceive the feelings that the music awakens in you. Try not to think about where you heard it before or what it reminds you of. Determine the kind of music you like to listen to and what mood you are in then. You can alter your mood by changing the music you listen to. Remember that music gives energy.

## ACTIVITY 6: Faces with feeling

Which face best reflects the feeling you are presently experiencing? Mark it. Have you experienced another feeling today which is reflected by another of the faces? Mark that one as well.

## Ways in which you can enhance your emotional awareness.

The following activities can enhance your emotional awareness:

- Keep a journal of your feelings. Indicate which situation gives rise to which feeling and what your reactions are. Become aware of the physical symptoms of your feelings – stiff neck, sweating, heart palpitations, etc. What emotion are you experiencing and what gave rise to it?
- Draw up a list of the roles you have and determine the feelings that are associated with each role, e.g.

employee (frustration), housewife (fulfilled), student (anxiety), etc.
- Try to generate feelings. In this way you can imagine which feelings you will experience in which situation and what your reaction to it will be. If you have to deliver a presentation soon, experience the situation and feelings beforehand in a safe place through visualisation. Visualisation is discussed in Chapter 5 in more detail.
- By keeping a journal of your dreams, you can become aware of unprocessed feelings in your subconscious mind. It is the feelings in your dreams that are important and not the situation in which they occur.

## ACTIVITY 7: Journal – situation/emotion/action

|  | Situation | Emotion | Action / Behaviour |
|---|---|---|---|
| Monday | | | |
| Tuesday | | | |
| Wednesday | | | |
| Thursday | | | |
| Friday | | | |
| Saturday | | | |
| Sunday | | | |

## ACTIVITY 8: Week of emotions: recognising and naming the important emotions in yourself and others

| Person | Mon | Tues | Wednes | Thurs | Fri | Sat | Sun |
|---|---|---|---|---|---|---|---|
| Self: | | | | | | | |
| Important other: | | | | | | | |
| Important other: | | | | | | | |
| Important other: | | | | | | | |

You can plan to fulfil your unmet needs when you see a pattern in your feelings. We tend to overemphasise our negative feelings and to see our positive feelings as less important. Make sure that you indicate your positive feelings as well, as these point to your fulfilled needs which are positive to you and which you have to keep as part of your life.

## ACTIVITY 9: Evaluate your own facial expression

Stand in front of a mirror and try to show different feelings on your face, e.g. sadness, anger, happiness, etc. How does your face look most of the time? Which message do you convey? This is a significant way in which you can evaluate whether your facial expressions are clear for others to read. Your negative body language sends negative messages to others. Are you aware of your nonverbal communication? Are you able to read other people's facial expressions?

## ACTIVITY 10: Developing your feeling vocabulary

See how many feeling words you can write down in three minutes, in order to determine what your feeling vocabulary is. Read the list of feelings (see p. 26) again.

### How can I understand feelings better?

Looking at the following can enhance insight into feelings:
* Certain situations give rise to certain feelings. If you always cry at weddings, you can prepare yourself by taking enough tissues!
* Different feelings may be experienced in the same situation. You may feel sad and satisfied in one situation. Take a funeral for example. If the person was seriously ill and suffered a lot of pain, you may be contented that the person is now without pain. That does not relieve your grief for the person though. Another example of this is when your husband wins a bursary to study overseas. You may be very pleased for him, but sad because you have to stay behind.

* Certain emotions belong together, e.g. uncertainty, inferiority, fear.
* Emotion can intensify, e.g. upset → angry → furious.
* By reading books (fiction) and watching movies, you can improve your knowledge of feelings.

## ACTIVITY 11: Feelings that go together

Which of the following feelings belong with the first feeling? (Underline the feelings which belong together in different colours.)

1. Love: jealousy, respect, guilt, trust.

2. Loneliness: depression, anger, dejection, discomfort.

3. Anger: irritated, thankful, frustrated.

4. Excited: cheerful, helpless, afraid, ecstatic.

### Primary and secondary feelings

The first basic feeling that you experience is the primary feeling, e.g. hurt. The primary feeling is often disguised/unclear, which means that you do not realise that you are experiencing it unless you take pains to identify it. When the secondary feelings like anger, aggression and sadness appear, you have to ask yourself: "What gave rise to these feelings?" It is very important to distinguish between primary and secondary feelings, as it is the primary feelings that indicate to you your unmet emotional needs. Knowing your unmet needs, you may plan to get them fulfilled, e.g. by asking for more attention/love if you have a need for some pampering: "I want you to hold me in your arms." Another example of this is when you feel depressed (secondary feeling). The primary feeling may be one of loneliness and the unmet emotional need may be to socialise and/or communicate.

## Intensity of feelings

It is important to first identify the primary feeling before you determine its intensity. Determining the correct intensity of a feeling is important because exaggeration or minimisation distorts the message you want to convey and undermines effective communication. You can do the following to express intensity:

- Use a word to describe the feeling: "I feel a little hurt" or "I feel very hurt."
- Use a word on the continuum of that feeling: upset, angry, furious.
- Use a scale of 1-10 to describe the intensity of the feeling: "I feel sad – about 5 out of 10."

Look at the example on this and the following page.

## Use of emotions

Using your emotions helps with reasoning and making better decisions. A decision about which you have positive feelings is often the correct decision, but you have to take the facts into consideration (think logically about it). Never make an important decision while you are experiencing strong feelings like anger. Emotions influence problem-solving. Don't ignore strong gut feelings about something. Use your gut feelings to prepare yourself and to inquire about the viability of an idea. Although intuition does not replace your good judgement, it strengthens it. A gut feeling may be a word, thought or image of which you become aware. Intuition may prepare you for an unpleasant situation. It is easier to recognise your gut feelings if you do not have rigid values, beliefs and opinions.

If you are more aware of your own feelings, you will be more aware of those of other people. This enables you to see different perspectives. Someone who has empathy with others is in contact with his feelings. Remember that you control your feelings and that you are responsible for your feelings and reactions.

**EXAMPLES OF INTENSITY OF FEELINGS**

1. Contented

2. Happy

3. Ecstatic

1. Annoyed

2. Angry

3. Furious

## ACTIVITY 12: To divide feelings according to intensity, primary and secondary feelings, and the roles you fulfil*

Evaluate your knowledge of feelings with this activity. An example is provided. After reading the list of feelings, try to divide it into groups, e.g. feelings relating to love, anger, motivation, etc. Of which intensity are they? Select approximately eight feelings.

| FEELINGS | MODERATE | STRONG | VERY STRONG |
|---|---|---|---|
| e.g. happy | feeling good | happy | elated |
| | | | |
| | | | |
| | | | |
| | | | |
| | | | |
| | | | |
| | | | |

Try to identify a few primary and secondary feelings.

| PRIMARY FEELINGS | SECONDARY FEELINGS |
| --- | --- |
| e.g. hurt as a result of an insult | anger, aggression |
|  |  |
|  |  |
|  |  |
|  |  |
|  |  |

Identify the roles you are involved with, e.g. spouse, breadwinner, housewife, mother/father, son/daughter, church leader, etc. and identify the feelings associated with each role.

| ROLES | FEELINGS |
| --- | --- |
| e.g. employee | proud, adequate, rebellious, afraid |
|  |  |
|  |  |
|  |  |
|  |  |
|  |  |
|  |  |

## ACTIVITY 13: Do you understand feelings?*

1. Indicate on a scale of 1-5 **how effective** the following reactions to the described situation would be, where 1 equals totally ineffective and 5 very effective.

### A. SITUATION

One of your friends phones to tell you some extremely good news about himself that he has just received.

### REACTION

(a) Congratulate him on the news.

(b) Ask him if he really deserved it.

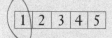

(c) Invite him over to listen to some music.

| 1 | 2 | 3 | 4 | 5 |

(d) Inquire whether there is anything with which you can assist him.

(e) Enjoy the moment with your friend.

(f) Any other answer:
_____
_____

## B. SITUATION

One of your colleagues looks upset. He asks you to go with him for a walk in the park. After a while he says that he would like to talk to you about his relationship with a married woman.

### REACTION

(a) Ask him about his feelings to enhance your understanding of the situation. Offer your assistance with no pressure from you.

`1 2 3 4 5`

(b) Entice him into giving you information about why he got involved with this woman. Try to suggest what he should do.

`1 2 3 4 5`

(c) Change the subject and say that it is inappropriate for him to discuss it with you.

`1 2 3 4 5`

(d) Tell him that you were in the same position and that you overcame the problem with the help of a therapist.

`1 2 3 4 5`

(e) Any other answer:
_____

## C. SITUATION

A friend phones and informs you that she has just received confirmation that she is terminally ill with lung cancer. She says that she is worried about her children.

### REACTION

(a) Show sympathy and tell her that you know someone else in the same situation to whom you can introduce her.

`1 2 3 4 5`

(b) There is nothing that you can do to change the situation, so distract her or change the subject.

`1 2 3 4 5`

(c) Tell her that you feel extremely sorry for her. Ask her to tell you what is happening and how she feels about it.

`1 2 3 4 5`

(d) Discuss her worries and her fears. Talk to her about what it means to her and how others coped with similar situations.

`1 2 3 4 5`

(e) Any other answer:
_____
_____

2. Indicate which of the actions/reactions mentioned below are the best **to cope with emotions.**

## A. SITUATION

You have just heard that 50% of your firm's staff are going to suffer a drastic reduction in salary as a result of a reduced working week. The final decision regarding which 50% it is going to be will be taken in a month's time.

**REACTION**

(a) You know the situation is still pending. As a final decision has still to be taken, you decide not to worry about it.

(b) Phone a friend and discuss the situation, hoping that he will make you feel better.

(c) Discuss it with friends and let them help you find a solution.

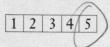

(d) You are too shocked to talk about it.

1 | 2 | 3 | 4 | 5

(e) Any other alternative:

_____

_____

## B. SITUATION

You found a cigarette in your child's pocket. When you confronted him with it, he denied that he had been smoking. As his clothes smelt of smoke, you confined him to the house for a month. Later you discovered that he was telling the truth.

**REACTION**

(a) Console yourself with the fact that parents sometimes make mistakes and leave it at that.

1 | 2 | 3 | 4 | 5

(b) Tell your child that you made a mistake, even though your intentions were good. Explain why you feel so strongly about it and apologise. Discuss how you will avoid similar situations in future.

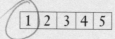

(c) Apologise; tell him that you are prepared to make amends and that you will consent to a reasonable request from him.

1 | 2 | 3 | 4 | 5

(d) Any other reaction:

_____

_____

### 3. The use of emotions

(a) Visualise a situation in which you experienced feelings of jealousy. When you can feel it clearly, indicate in the table below how you feel about each category.

| Warm | | | | ✓ | | Cold |
|---|---|---|---|---|---|---|
| Dark | ✓ | | | | | Light |
| Low | ✓ | | | | | High |
| Orange | ✓ | | | | | Blue |
| Fast | ✓ | | | | | Slow |
| Sharp | ✓ | | | | | Blunt |
| Happy | | | | ✓ | | Unhappy |

| Good | | | | | ✓ | Bad |
|------|--|--|--|--|---|-----|
| Sweet | | | | | ✓ | Sour |
| Yellow | | ✓ | | | | Purple |

(b) A very capable colleague at work pays you an unexpected compliment. How do you feel about her? Indicate which emotions you will experience.

| Comfortable | |
|-------------|--|
| Calm | |
| Guilty | |
| Optimistic | ✓ |
| Imaginative | |
| Proud | ✓ |
| Surprised | ✓ |
| Trusting | |
| Energetic | |
| Sceptical | |

Any other: _FULFILLED_

## 4. Understand emotions

Emotions can be understood on different levels and in different ways. Indicate with an appropriate example whether the following are true or untrue.

(a) Emotions are sometimes simple and sometimes complex, as one emotion can be a combination of two or more feelings.

| (True) | Untrue |

Example: _GUILT = simply you feel responsible & bad. The event may not have been intended. You feel remorse and a need to repay_

(b) Emotions can progressively intensify.

[ (True) ] [ Untrue ]

Example: I feel sad → inadequate → deeply unhappy → hate for myself → hurt myself

(c) Two people can interpret the same emotion differently and react to it differently.

[ (True) ] [ Untrue ]

Example: Mick feels anger. He takes it out on me (Mick's reaction) I feel anger. I feel ashamed & take it out on myself.

(d) The results of the expression of one emotion (e.g. anger) can lead to another feeling.

[ (True) ] [ Untrue ]

Example: I am envious, I act piqued → then feel guilty for feeling that.

## ACTIVITY 14: Combine feelings to gain a better understanding of how a combination can work

|  | Happy | Angry | Pleased | Satisfied |
|---|---|---|---|---|
| Sad | x |  |  |  |
| Uncertain |  |  |  |  |
| Shocked |  |  |  |  |
| Surprised |  |  |  |  |

Combine the different feelings randomly and ask yourself the following questions:

1. How can I be happy while I am sad?

I am sad Ann is dying but happy her death is quick.

2. Is it possible to be angry and surprised at the same time?

*I can be suprised at the intensity of my anger*

3. In which situation can I be sad and satisfied simultaneously?

*I was sad at Franks funeral but satisfied I did my best in giving the address*

Try to imagine different situations in which contradictory feelings appear at the same time.

*You can be pleased a friend won a prize but shocked because you thought it could be better done to win*

## SUMMARY

This chapter is very important as it presents the basics of emotional intelligence and thus the foundation of this book. Feelings are an inseparable part of each person. It is important to be able to reason logically and to solve problems cognitively. However, it is equally important to be in touch with your "heart", that is your feelings. Enhance your emotional awareness by paying attention to the physical changes in your body. Determine the effect which external things like buildings and colours have on your emotions.

It is very important to keep a feeling journal for at least two months in order to become aware of certain tendencies.

The following chapter is as important as this one. In the discussion of values and assumptions, it is important that you know what they are and that you can identify them in your life.

# CHAPTER 2
## the role of values and assumptions

The focus is now on your values and assumptions, in other words on what guides your inner humanity and your life. We often do what we believe is correct for the sake of relationships, the values/expectations of the community or just to survive. We seldom question our beliefs and actions. Sometimes something has to happen before we start to evaluate our lives. We are forced to question who we are and what our goals and values are. Frequently we don't know the answers, or perhaps we have no goals or meaning in our lives. It is only when we know what our values and beliefs are that we can plan effectively to take responsibility for our lives.

Put some effort into understanding this section, as we often refer to your values and assumptions in the workbook. Firstly, we focus on values.

## VALUES

Your values form the core of your humanity. Most people never think about this and they find it hard to determine the values that guide their lives. Think about the following questions:

What am I striving for?
On what do I spend money?
How do I pass my time?
What do I regard as important?
What guides my life?

If you strive for the "correct" values, you experience health and happiness. If you strive for the "wrong" values, you have the wrong goals and you experience an unfulfilled life. You may be unhappy even if you reach your goals. An example of this is a person who gives everything to start his own business only to realise eventually that that is not what he really wanted.

What are the "right" and the "wrong" values? It depends on the priority you give to certain values. A healthy value may have a negative influence on your life if you are too dependent on it, e.g. competition (to always compete and be the winner).

Values of "giving" and "being" are usually positive values, while values of "receiving" may be more negative. Values which you can control (giving and being), give you more pleasure, as you are not dependent on someone else giving them to you. On the other hand, those values that you cannot control may result in more negative feelings. If you highly value recognition from others, you may often be disappointed as other people are in control of giving that to you. It is a fact that people do not give recognition easily. Values guide us in what we want to achieve/have. They are learnt early in life and may be transferred from generation to generation. These values are not easily questioned. They are often so embedded that they cannot be changed without effort. However, values can be changed, and you may exchange them for values which hold more positive feelings for you. It is your responsibility to:

1. Determine the values that guide your life;
2. Evaluate them in terms of the consequences they have for you, and
3. Decide which to change and which to leave as is.

Mostly we suffer from an unhealthy and dysfunctional prioritisation of values.

# ACTIVITY 15: Values

Indicate which values are important to you. Tick those that bring you positive feelings and use a cross for the values that lead to negative feelings.

| | | | |
|---|---|---|---|
| Academic achievement | ✓ | Exploitation | ✗ |
| Acceptance | ✓ | Freedom | ✓ |
| Admiration | ✓ | Perfectionism | ✓ |
| Appearances | ✓ | Self-control | ✓ |
| Approval | ✓ | Organisation | ✓ |
| Attention | ✓ | Achievement | ✓ |
| Authority | ✗ | Avoidance of pain | ✓ |
| Cleanliness | ✓ | Peacefulness | ✓ |
| Communication | ✓ | Recognition | ✓ |
| Competition | ✓ | Self-fulfilment | ✓ |
| Conformity | ✗ | Aggressiveness | ✗ |
| Co-operation | ✓ | Relationships | ✓ |
| Distraction | ✓ | Reality | ✓ |
| Education | ✓ | Respect for others | ✓ |
| Unconditional love | ✓ | Security | ✓ |
| Others' view/opinion | ✓ | Self-devotion | ✗ |
| Popularity | ✓ | Efficiency | ✓ |
| Good manners | ✓ | Entertainment | ✓ |
| Material wealth | ✓ | Equality | ✓ |
| Image | ✓ | Expression | ✓ |
| Independence | ✓ | Religion | ✗ |
| Independent thinking | ✓ | Friendship | ✓ |
| Integrity | ✓ | Happiness | ✓ |

| | | | |
|---|---|---|---|
| Knowledge | ✓ | Hard work | ✓ |
| Courage | ✓ | Compassion | ✓ |
| Responsibility | ✓ | Honesty | ✓ |
| Self-discipline | ✓ | Logic/reason | ✓ |
| Balance | ✓ | Loyalty | ✓ |
| Trustworthiness | ✓ | Moral awareness | ✓ |
| Suspicion | ✗ | Unselfishness | ✓ |
| Harmony | ✓ | Stability | ✓ |
| Growth | ✓ | Sensitivity | ✓ |
| Health | ✓ | Friendliness | ✓ |
| Care for others | ✓ | Justice | ✓ |
| Optimism | ✓ | Mercifulness | ✓ |
| Appreciation | ✓ | Humanity | ✓ |
| Performance | ✓ | Success | ✓ |
| To make a difference | ✓ | Self-respect | ✓ |
| Perseverance | ✓ | Prestige | ✓ |
| Selfishness | ✗ | Mistrust | ✗ |
| Egotism | ✗ | Fairness | ✓ |
| Power | ✗ | Suspicion | ✗ |

## ACTIVITY 16: Value cards[8]

Make a copy of the ten value cards on the following two pages.
1. Cut them out and prioritise them from most important to least important as they are in your life at the moment. What have you learnt from this?
2. Hold the cards face down in your hand. Take any five and put them aside. Which five do you still have? Can you function effectively with these five values?
3. Take the three cards you regard as most important. How much time do you spend on these values? (Look at the activity analysis – Activity 42 – in the next chapter.)

Religion/Wisdom

Family

Peacefulness

Communication

Beauty

Friendship

Balance

Money

Acceptance/Popularity

Independence

## ASSUMPTIONS, PRECONCEPTIONS AND PREJUDICES

A person's assumptions, preconceptions and preju-dices (core beliefs) can be described as his "truth", his belief about how things work and ought to work. These convictions are learnt from early childhood onwards and form a large part of a person's make-up. People are brought up with certain preconceived ideas with which they test life. When their life does not resemble their expectations or ideas, they find it difficult to cope. They form quite an extended part of human life, and people find it very difficult to think that these beliefs can be questioned and changed. Can you answer the following questions?

**What do I believe about**
Relationships . . .
Needs . . .
The world . . .
My rights . . .
The roles I play . . .
Mistakes . . .
Feelings . . .
Problems . . .
Trust . . .

Assumptions are usually the result of absolutist thinking about yourself, others and the world (e.g. "The world is bad"). These rigid ways of thinking lead to assumptions such as: "If something bad can happen in this situation, it will happen to me" or "I must be the best in everything in order for other people to accept me" or "I should not say too much because others will notice how little I know." More examples of this will be given later.

Test your negative deep-seated assumptions as hypotheses – take all the information into account: all words, situations and events which could prove that you are accepted even when you are not the best. Experiment in order to prove your assumptions incorrect. Look at the way people react to you in testing the assumption "I am without value." When you accept a new assumption e.g., "I am valuable," be open to facts which prove this correct, such as people greeting you, caring about you or your doing something of value for another person. Start with a low-risk assumption and test it.

A new assumption may be the opposite of the old one or the absolutist assumption may be qualified; for instance: "I find it difficult to cope with new situations, but I am able to if I really try." It takes time to believe in a new assumption.

Be on the lookout for evidence (events/experiences) from your past which prove your new assumption to be correct. It may be that people have always talked to you easily and cared about you, but that you have lost sight of this. Your assumptions and convictions have developed over a long time and they may take a long time to change. The first step is just to realise that they might be wrong! It is important to get to the bottom of your assumptions. You can do this by asking yourself a few questions about them, e.g. **"I should not say too much because others will realise how little I know."** Ask yourself: If that is true, what will happen? → **"They will not like me."** If that is true what will happen? → **"They will ignore me."** If that is true what will happen? → **"I will be alone and will feel rejected."** Do this until you come to the heart of it in order for you to do something about it or to realise how irrational your assumption is.

## CONVICTIONS/ASSUMPTIONS/ PREJUDICES

## ARE LEARNT BY

## CONDITIONING
(Continuous reinforcement and repetition)

## WHICH LEADS TO

## CERTAIN EXPECTATIONS

## WHICH HAVE CERTAIN

## BEHAVIOUR AS A RESULT. THIS BEHAVIOUR BECOMES A HABIT.

If you live according to a certain frame of reference, e.g. "I will always have problems and will never be successful," you'll have the expectation that this will always be true. Everything which happens around you and to you will be seen from this perspective and you will only see that which confirms your expectations. You will ignore the positive events or think of reasons why they are not applicable to you. You only believe in what you want to believe and what proves your convictions to be true. When your employer gives you a compliment you will reject it with various reasons as to why he did it, e.g. "He wants something from me."

"Be careful what you look for because you will find it."
*Anonymous*

Positive assumptions give energy to enjoy yourself and your relationships. Look carefully at the following quotation from Victor Frankl:

"I discovered the ultimate freedom, the ability to choose your attitude irrespective of circumstance."

The following quotation relates to this as well:

"Attitude is the mind's paintbrush – it can colour any situation."
*Anonymous*

Your interpretations regarding situations/events are strongly influenced by the assumptions/convictions that you have. Irrational assumptions give rise to negative interpretations. The fewer irrational assumptions you have, the more energy you will have to enjoy yourself and your friends. Irrational assumptions are learnt early in life. They are like a bad habit that can be unlearnt.

## ACTIVITY 17: Assumptions*

Read the following general assumptions[9] and decide which of them describe how you feel. Re-read them and indicate which are rational and which irrational.

*IRRAT* 1. Everybody must always like me, love me and approve of my actions otherwise I feel absolutely miserable and totally useless.

*RAT* 2. It would be pleasant if everybody liked me, but I can survive without the approval of most people. It is only the approval of close friends and people with "power" over me (like my employer) about which I should be concerned.

*I FEEL IRRAT* 3. I have to be perfect and competent in all respects before I will regard myself as worth something.

*RAT* 4. My personal values do not depend on how perfect or competent I am. Although I try to be as competent as possible, I am a valuable person irrespective of how well I do things.

*IRR* 5. People who are bad, like myself, should be blamed and punished to prevent them from doing bad things in future.

*IRR* 6. It is important not to repeat the same mistakes in future. I need not blame or punish myself for what happened in the past.

*I FEEL* 7. It is a total catastrophe and so intolerable that I cannot bear it if things are not the way I want them to be.

*RAT* 8. There is no reason why the world should be the way I want it to be. It is important to cope with life as it is. I should not complain about the fact that things are not just or the way I want them to be.

*IRRAT* 9. If there is a possibility that something really bad might happen, I will constantly think about it as if it is indeed going to happen.

*RAT* 10. I will do my best to avoid future unpleasantness. Thereafter I will not concern myself about anything. I refuse to be frightened by the question: "What if it happens?"

*IRRAT* 11. It is easier to avoid problems and the responsibility they entail than to cope with them.

*I feel RAT* 12. In the long run it is easier/better to cope with problems and the responsibility they entail than to avoid them.

*I feel RAT* 13. I need someone stronger than myself to rely on.

*I feel IRRAT* 14. I am strong enough to rely on myself.

*IRRAT* 15. I have been like this since childhood and I can't change.

*I feel RAT* 16. I can change myself at any stage during my life when I decide that it is in my interest to do so.

*IRRAT* 17. I should get miserable and depressed when other people have problems.

*I feel RAT* 18. To help other people and to

have empathy with them does not mean that I should get depressed about it or get involved in their problems. How can I help them if I am depressed myself?

*...I.R.R.A.T* 19. It is bad and unbearable if I have to do things that I do not want or like to do.

*...I feel RAT* 20. I will not allow things that I cannot change to upset me.

## ACTIVITY 18: Formulate an assumption

What is your immediate assumption when you hear the following: (Be honest!)

• I want to emigrate:

*I wonder what is so bad in their life? Being in different country may not change that*

• I want to change jobs:

*I hope they realise how scarce jobs are at present*

• I want to see a cosmetic surgeon:

*They are vain & wasteful of money (will that change things to better their life?)*

Look at the above assumptions. Are they generally negative and prejudiced? Try to reformulate at least one of them if it is negative and prejudiced.

_____

_____

_____

*Examples of assumptions, negative thoughts and preconceptions that may influence your life drastically* [10]

| | |
|---|---|
| *I am an awful person . . .* | *(Self-criticism)* |
| That was not good enough . . . | (I am not easily satisfied) |
| This is your mistake . . . *IF IT IS* | (Always blaming someone else) |
| *I AM WORRIED ABOUT EVERYTHING . . .* | (PESSIMISM) |
| *I don't like compliments . . .* | *(They make me uncomfortable)* |
| *I can't . . .* | *(I am not willing to try anything new or different)* |
| I can't do it again . . . | (One success does not mean there are more to come) |

I HAVE TO HAVE MORE, RECEIVE MORE . . .

(ALWAYS STRIVING FOR MORE)

I am always anxious about something . . .

(Uneasy feeling about everything)

I ALWAYS AGREE WITH THE GROUP,
OR SOMEONE ELSE . . .

(I DON'T HAVE AN OPINION)

I don't allow anyone to mess with me . . .

(Attack, insult easily, do not have a lot of self-respect)

I say what I want to say . . .

(I don't care too much about others' feelings)

How do I compare?

(I always compare myself to someone else)

You have a lot of shortcomings as well . . .

(Now I can accept mine more easily)

I am responsible for other people's happiness . . .

(We are responsible for our own happiness)

Everyone has to like me . . .

(Or else I am not worth much)

I am very fragile, sensitive . . .

(People should handle me with care)

I often feel "out", not part
of the group . . .

(I am not yet aware of my unique
ness)

I have to be the best . . .

(Or else I know I am not good enough)

People misuse me . . .

(I do a lot for other people)

I don't need help from anyone . . .

(I'd rather struggle on my own)

My world would end if you left
me or if you died . . .

(Overdependent)

It is not fair that . . .

(Judgement according to your standards)

## ACTIVITY 19: Identify your negative assumptions and formulate an alternative for each

It is very important for you to recognise and reformulate your own negative assumptions. In this way you can see events and situations in a different light. Begin your negative assumptions with, e.g., "I am . . .", "I should . . . ", "Other people are . . . ", "Other people should . . . ", "The world is . . . " or "The world should . . . " Begin your alternative assumptions with the following words: "If I really want to, I can . . . " or "I am not hopeless, I can try my best to cope with it" or "My best is good enough" or "I can do it. I may feel afraid, I just have to relax."

1. Negative assumption:
_____
_____

Alternative assumption:
_____
_____

2. Negative assumption:
_____
_____

Alternative assumption:
_____
_____

3. Negative assumption:
_____
_____

Alternative assumption:
_____
_____

4. Negative assumption:
_____
_____

Alternative assumption:
_____
_____

5. Negative assumption:
_____
_____

Alternative assumption:
_____
_____

### Values and assumptions determine emotional needs

Our values and assumptions determine our emotional needs and expectations, as they show us what we want to experience, receive or give. What are emotional needs? They are, *inter alia*: recognition, love, consolation, acceptance, friendship, admiration, peace, freedom, silence and respect.

### Emotional needs lead to feelings

The feelings we experience are to a large extent the result of our emotional needs. If we do not receive what we strive for, we feel frustrated, unfulfilled and unhappy. Unmet emotional needs lead therefore to negative feelings. For example, if you say, "I feel abused or neglected" the unmet emotional needs are recognition and appreciation. If you feel lonely, you may have a need for socialising. You may have a need for silence and privacy if you feel overwhelmed among people. In the same way positive feelings come from fulfilled emotional needs, e.g. it is my need to do something for someone. If I have visited a person in the hospital, I feel satisfied and thankful.

### How can I feel more fulfilled?

To experience more positive feelings and fewer negative feelings, you have to explore your values and assumptions. Be prepared to change your perspective (views and expectations) about life if that will make you feel more fulfilled. Try to keep a journal for a period of time to become aware of the feelings you experience most often. These feelings may show your unmet emotional needs and your negative values and assumptions. They may also give you an indication of your needs that are met.

Remember that we tend to extend our unpleasant experiences and to think about them for a long time. If you keep a journal of your feelings, you may become aware that you have experienced just as many positive feelings, but that you have given more attention to the negative ones. We tend to experience our negative situations more intensely than we do our positive situations. Learn to enjoy your positive experiences intensely and to prolong them!

With regard to the chart below, consider the following: your values and assumptions are the foundation of your needs (that which you want to experience, give and receive) as well as your feelings, whether or not the needs are fulfilled. All emotions, even "nega-tive" emotions, are seen as good because they indicate your unmet needs. Therefore you have the responsibility to plan the fulfilment of your needs.

We all have needs and these needs change continuously. If you have a good emotional awareness, you will be able to recognise these needs and provide for them. The better you know your needs and are able to get them fulfilled, the more positive emotions you may experience. Below are examples of needs you may have in your present situation.

## Where do feelings come from?

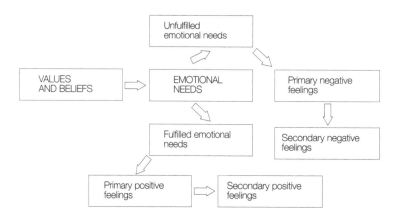

## ACTIVITY 20: Needs

Tick the needs you have to give more attention to and try to fulfil them.

| Need: (in your public life) | | | |
|---|---|---|---|
| Safety/security | | Excitement | |
| To investigate things | | Freedom | |
| Information | | Access (e.g. to transport, library, etc.) | |
| Citizenship of a country | | Skills (such as how to buy tickets) | |
| Status | | Knowledge (where to go/what to avoid) | |
| Peace | | A community to belong to | |

**Need: (in your social and working environment)**

| | | | |
|---|---|---|---|
| Activity (work and play) | | Successful performance | |
| Competency (I can . . . ) | | Respect | |
| Involvement | | Fun | |
| Group interaction | | Planning | |
| Health/diet/sleep | | Exercise | |
| Socialising (relationships) | | Social support system | |
| Discharge (talk about feelings) | | Lifestyle management | |
| Decision-making | | Recognition | |

**Need: (in your personal life)**

| | | | |
|---|---|---|---|
| Closeness | | Sharing of feelings and thoughts | |
| Growth | | Self-knowledge | |
| Happiness | | Self-assertiveness | |
| Caring for yourself | | To take care of others | |
| Friends | | Community (We are the same . . . ) | |
| Respect | | Equality | |
| Recognition | | Purpose and meaning | |
| Acceptance | | Boundaries (You are there and I am here.) | |

**Need: (in your intimate life)**

| | | | |
|---|---|---|---|
| Love | | To be understood | |
| Trust | | Altruism (to do good to others) | |
| Bonding | | Spiritual knowledge (religion) | |
| Sensual and sexual needs | | Withdrawal (I want to think.) | |
| Cherishing | | Privacy (I want to be alone.) | |

It is important to remember that everyone has the following five components: emotional/psychological, intellectual, physical, spiritual/religious, social. You have to strive for balance in fulfilling your needs on all the levels. Some needs are more important than others (according to the needs hierarchy of Maslow).

## ACTIVITY 21: To identify feelings, values, assumptions and needs from events which caused negative feelings*

Read the following paragraph:

"Last week I had a very bad experience. I worked for hours on a presentation I had to make, but then my boss told me during the meeting that it was not good enough. I was extremely upset! I really did my best and thought that the presentation would be well accepted. My boss is not fair. He has his favourites and I am not one of them. I still believe that my presentation was one of the best."

Then complete the following:

1. Which feelings did the person experience? Try to identify five.

*embarassment / dejection / failure*

2. Which values did the person have?

*self - ego / perfectionism*

3. Which needs of the person were not fulfilled or were overlooked?

*pride / effort*

4. Name a few of the person's irrational beliefs.

*inferiority*

Have you ever realised that your thoughts have a direct influence on your feelings and behaviour? In the next section we focus on the role your thoughts play in your life.

## THE IMPORTANT ROLE OF THOUGHTS IN YOUR EMOTIONS

Thoughts lead to feelings. Many of the feelings you experience were preceded by a thought, no matter how short, momentary or unnoticed it was. Situations themselves often do not have emotional content – it is your interpretations which give rise to your feelings. If you tend to think negative thoughts you will experience negative emotions. Someone who thinks that he is not worth anything may experience feelings of inferiority and uncertainty. A person thinks up to 1 200 thoughts per minute – make sure that they are constructive!

You can control your emotions by changing your thinking patterns. There is much truth in the sayings: **"You are what you think"** and **"Your life depends on your thoughts."** Your thoughts reflect your inner world. What you think and how you guide your thinking is a choice that you make from moment to moment. If you are unable to guide your thoughts you are unable to guide your life. Don't try to change your thoughts to positive ones – develop alternative or balanced thinking. If you continually think that you can't do something, it will not help just to tell yourself, "I can do it," because you will not really believe yourself. A positive statement in itself will not lead to positive feelings or behaviour. A better alternative is this: "It will be difficult for me, but I can give it a try. If I don't succeed I can try something different." This will reassure you much more and you will feel more motivated.

It may be explained as follows:

**A = Event (situation), B = Thoughts and C = Feelings and behaviour**

Your task is to change **B** in order to have a different **C**.

Certain thoughts may lead to certain feelings that again may give rise to certain thoughts. These further thoughts reinforce or support the initial feelings.

An example of the succession and reinforcement between thoughts and feelings is as follows:

↓ **Thought:** "Nobody wants to talk to me."

↓ **Feeling:** Disappointed

↓ **Thought:** "They all ignore me."

↓ **Feeling:** Sadness

↓ **Thought:** "I want to go home and be alone."

↓ **Feeling:** Dejected

↓ **Thought:** "I am not worth anything."

→ **Feeling:** Depressed

Can you see how the negative thoughts succeed each other and how the feeling intensifies? The stronger the feeling, the more extreme the thoughts, e.g. anxious people see danger in everything, no matter how small or innocent. A cycle is formed where the feelings and thoughts feed and maintain each other. It is essential that you recognise and control these thoughts in yourself as soon as possible, so as to experience more positive feelings.

You might think: "I feel afraid. If I did not have reason to be afraid, I would not have experienced the feeling." By doing this you confirm the feeling but not the facts. Thus, make certain of the facts before you draw any conclusions. Don't confuse feelings of fear with intuition. Be aware of what you say to yourself and what you think. Your brain is like a computer that you programme. If you programme yourself negatively, you limit yourself as to what you can do. Any positive feedback is reacted upon negatively, because you are programmed to do so. When you experience intense feelings you will ignore or distort any information which is contradictory to your feelings. Someone who suffers from depression will not recognise a helping hand or make use of it. He may have various excuses why the other person is not able to help him. Another example of this is when someone who usually feels inferior receives a compliment. His brain will not process the information because it is not programmed to hear positive things about himself.

When you want to change your behaviour or want to learn new behaviour, it depends on your thoughts whether you will succeed or not. Your expectations determine your reactions. In most cases positive expectations will lead to positive behaviour. For example, if you expect to realise a dream, you will work very hard to accomplish just that.

### Automatic and distorted thinking patterns

You begin to control your negative unpleasant feelings by becoming aware of your automatic thoughts. When you experience an unpleasant feeling, ask yourself: "What did I think of just before experiencing this feeling?" Your assumptions/"core beliefs" determine your automatic thoughts. You are usually not aware of these thoughts and it is important to become aware of them. They are frequently irrational, spontaneous and uncensored. The intensity of the thought mirrors the intensity of the feeling. Although you may not always be aware of the thought, you believe in it. The thought can be very cryptic, e.g. "Liar!" if someone tells you something. One automatic thought may lead to another and it may be repetitive. What you say is often different from what you think.

## ACTIVITY 22: Identify your distorted thinking patterns

Some examples of negative, distorted thinking patterns, which lead to negative feelings and incomplete perspectives, follow. Can you identify them in yourself? Reformulate your distorted thoughts where applicable.

| Distorted thoughts | Description | Reformulate your thoughts |
|---|---|---|
| Exaggeration | You exaggerate the importance of problems in your life or you minimise the importance of good things in your life. | |
| Reading another's thoughts | You expect others to read your mind or you try to do it with other people. | |
| White-or-black thinking | An all-or-nothing attitude, e.g. something has to be right or wrong with no other alternatives, possibilities or compromises. | |
| Take over | You choose a negative situation and think about it excessively. The reality then looks dark and hopeless. It is difficult for you to see the positive side of a situation. | |
| Ignore the positive | You ignore anything positive and never give yourself or anyone else recognition for work well done. | |
| Irrational expectations | E.g. "Everyone has to like me." | |
| Labels | "I am a loser." "He is a liar." | |
| Blaming | You always blame yourself or others. | |
| Generalisation | You generalise one (bad) experience to all other experiences. | |
| Rules of behaviour | You have specific expectations about the behaviour of people. If they do not live up to them, you feel dejected. | |
| Prediction of the future | You predict the future in a negative way. You predict that negative events will occur. | |
| Feelings are reality* | Your feelings are not based of facts, but you accept your feelings as real. It may be the result of a wrong interpretation. | |
| Catastrophic thinking | You always expect the worst that can happen in any situation. | |

| Distorted thoughts | Description | Reformulate your thoughts |
|---|---|---|
| Ought to | Any thought starting with: "I/he/she ought to . . ." | |
| Personification | You think you are personally responsible for all events (even earthquakes and floods) and you feel guilty about them. You always compare yourself with others. | |
| Filters | You filter the facts and only believe those which you believe to be applicable to you. | |

*To feel afraid does not mean that you have reason to be afraid. An example of this is: a person taps you on the shoulder and tells you that there is a snake behind you. Depending on the way you interpret the situation, you either think that the person is joking or that he is telling the truth. In the first instance you will feel relaxed, but in the second instance you will be frightened and jump away. Your reaction (do nothing or jump away) will depend on your feelings (relaxed or afraid) before you know whether there is a snake or not.

If some of these thinking patterns are present in a very serious way, it may be an indication that the person is suffering from a psychological disorder and that he needs help from a professional therapist. An example of the manner in which automatic thoughts succeed each other is the following:

↓ "I'll gladly go to the party."

↓ "But I don't have anything appropriate to wear."

↓ "Everyone will be dressed to perfection."

↓ "And my hair needs cutting."

↓ "Maybe I should stay at home and read a book."

↓ "Nobody will miss me anyway."

→ "I am worthless."

You may have automatic thoughts while you talk to someone:

↓ "Liar!"

↓ "That story again!"

↓ "It is not true."

↓ "You only think about yourself."

→ "It makes me sick."

Consider the thought which leads to the strong feelings within you as a hypothesis that should be proved as correct or incorrect. (As you did with your assumptions – see p. 49.) Evidence consists of facts, data and information and not your own interpretations. Additional information can change your interpretation of a situation to a large degree. Therefore you have to gather as much information as possible before you come to a conclusion. Do you have evidence for that which you believe in? Ask for more information or confirmation before you react in order to be sure that your reaction is the correct response in the specific situation.

Try to formulate alternative thoughts as soon as you recognise one of the distorted thinking patterns in yourself, e.g. "If I can't do it correctly, I should not try." (All or nothing.) Reformulate it as follows: "I shall try to do it correctly. If it is not right, at least I have tried." If you tend to read other people's minds or assume that you know what they are feeling, resolve that you will never again come to conclusions about their thoughts or feelings without confirming with them. When you are having catastrophic thoughts stop and ask yourself what the chances are that your fears will come true. If you have rules about the behaviour of other people, remember that your values are different from those of other people, that every person is unique and that their behaviour is their choice.

If you believe the alternative thought, the intensity of the negative feeling will decrease and you may experience heightened energy levels. See it as an experiment. Remember that your assumptions and beliefs are the foundation of your thoughts. By becoming aware of your thoughts you are getting to know your assumptions. These two components are closely related. If you can change your thinking patterns, you can change your assumptions and vice versa. Embedded thinking patterns may be changed through visualisation where you see yourself as you have formulated it in the alternative assumption. Use positive confirmations in your visualisation.

Your visualisation has to be
1. Positive
2. In the present tense
3. Possible/realistic for you.

E.g. "I am successful with . . . ", "I can do it if I really want to . . . "

The following activity will show you visually how powerful your thoughts are. It is very important that you realise the impact of your thoughts in order to start controlling them. Remember that each of your actions was once a thought and the beginning of a process to programme yourself. Thoughts are already energy. The clearer your thoughts (the picture in your visualisation), the more energy is radiated and the greater the possibility that your thoughts become reality. This is applicable to both positive and negative thoughts!

## ACTIVITY 23: The power of your thoughts

Put a piece of string through a paper clip. Draw a vertical and a horizontal line on a piece of paper. They should cross each other in the middle of the paper. Write on the upper part of the vertical line "North" and on the lower part "South". On the left-hand side of the horizontal line write "West" and the other side (right) "East". If you hold the string in your hand, the paper clip should hang just above the cross on the paper. Your elbow must be on the table. The distance between the paper clip and your hand should be about 25 cm. Keep the paper clip as motionless as possible. Now move the clip from north to south and then from west to east. Again hold it just above the cross. Visualise the motion of the paper clip, first from north to south without moving it with your hand. Repeat the thought in your mind until you see the movement. After you have seen it, stop using the paper clip and visualise the movement from west to east. Try it! You should be able to see a clear movement in the direction you have visualised. Our thoughts are extremely powerful!

## ACTIVITY 24: Unlearn negative automatic thoughts

Put a rubber band around your wrist and lightly "shoot" yourself with it each time you have a negative automatic thought. Later you will recognise the thought immediately. You will be able to stop yourself sooner and this will enable you to think an alternative thought. In this way you can transform your thoughts by not letting them go rampant. You will be able to guide them consciously in the direction of your choice.

### The relation between your thoughts and problems

It is frequently possible to see that your thoughts are at the root of your problems when you make an analysis of your problems and the emotions related to them. In the following problem analysis you have to give attention to the way in which the negative thoughts and assumptions lead to negative feelings. The alternative assumption leads to more positive feelings.

## Understand your problems

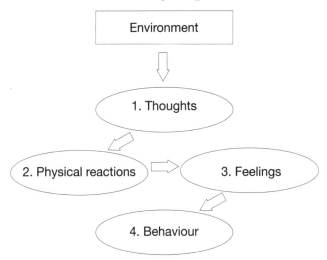

## EXAMPLE OF PROBLEM ANALYSIS

### ANXIETY
**Life situation:** Any important event in your life, e.g. trauma (accident, abuse) or something that you still have to do (make a presentation). Any recent change in your life.

**Thoughts:** Overestimating danger, underestimating your abilities to cope with a situation, underestimating the help available, worries and catastrophic thoughts. "What if . . . ?"

**Physical reactions:** Sweaty hands, muscle tension, heart palpitations, dizziness, insomnia, poor appetite.

**Feelings:** Tense, irritated, anxious, panic-stricken, afraid, inferior, unsure.

**Behaviour:** Avoidance of or withdrawing from certain situations, trying to be perfect because of fear of failure, wanting to have control of the situation, starting to drink or use drugs.

**Possible assumptions:** I can't cope with new situations, I can't do it alone, people always hurt me, the world is bad.

**Possible alternative assumptions:** If I really want to, I can do my best to adapt to a new situation. Although it may be difficult at first, I can do it on my own.

Is it possible for you to feel the relief which is related to the alternative assumption?

## ACTIVITY 25: Problem analysis

My own problem:
_____
_____

Life situation:
_____
_____

Thoughts:
_____
_____

Physical reactions:
_____
_____

Feelings:
_____
_____

Behaviour:
_____
_____

Possible assumptions:
_____
_____

Possible alternative assumptions:
_____
_____

## ACTIVITY 26: Thoughts and feelings

The purpose of this activity is to show you that in your own experiences your thoughts may give rise to certain physical symptoms and feelings.

1. What were your initial **thoughts** while you travelled for the first time to a situation which you regarded as stressful (work interview, examination, selection)?
_____
_____

2. What **physical reactions** did you experience in your body when you arrived there?

_____

_____

3. What were your initial **feelings** when you arrived there?

_____

_____

4. Did you start **thinking differently** about it after your arrival? What did you think?

_____

_____

5. What **physical reactions** did you experience afterwards?

_____

_____

6. Did your thoughts lead to **different feelings** within you? What were the feelings?

_____

_____

7. What did you **do** with the feelings that you experienced? (Suppressed, ignored, recognised, accepted, other.)

_____

_____

8. Can you recognise a negative **assumption/value/prejudice** that is related to your thoughts and feelings about the situation?

_____

_____

9. Formulate an alternative assumption in place of the above.

_____

_____

## ACTIVITY 27: The relation between situations and behaviour

The following table has to be completed for those **specific situations** in which you find yourself frequently, and afterwards you realise that you have not reacted appropriately. Can you identify distorted thinking patterns?

| Situation | Thoughts | Feelings | Reaction |
|---|---|---|---|
| Who?, what?, where?, etc. | What do I think? | Which feelings do I experience? | What is my reaction to my feelings? |
| 1. | | | |
| 2. | | | |
| 3. | | | |
| 4. | | | |
| 5. | | | |

Now do Activity 28 on the next page.

# ACTIVITY 28: Journal about automatic and alternative thoughts

| Situation:<br>Who?,<br>what?,<br>when?,<br>where?,<br>why? | Feeling<br>intensity<br>1-10 | Automatic<br>thought. Think before<br>and during situation | Irrational or<br>mistaken<br>thought pattern | Facts which<br>support the<br>thought pattern | Facts which<br>oppose the<br>thought pattern | Alternative<br>balanced<br>thoughts –<br>hypothesis | Feeling<br>intensity<br>1-10 |
|---|---|---|---|---|---|---|---|
| E.g.: Since<br>my divorce,<br>I don't trust<br>men. | Mistrust, 9 | – He will be disloyal.<br>– All men are dishonest. | Overgeneralisation | High %<br>divorces.<br>Few good<br>marriages. | All men are not<br>disloyal. Women<br>have a part in this.<br>My parents were<br>happily married. | I have to get to<br>know someone<br>before I can deter-<br>mine his trust-<br>worthiness | Uncertainty, 5<br>Mistrust, 2 |
| | | | | | | | |
| | | | | | | | |
| | | | | | | | |
| | | | | | | | |
| | | | | | | | |

## ACTIVITY 29: Improving emotional awareness

This activity is directed at making you aware of familiar situations with which you can identify and during which you experienced similar feelings. Page through a newspaper or watch the television news. Find a situation with which you can identify, e.g. divorce, financial need, etc. First ask yourself if you know anyone who went through such a situation. Then ask yourself whether **you yourself** have experienced the feelings of pain, hopelessness, anger, trauma, disgust or shock. If applicable, can you remember the physical symptoms or thinking patterns that preceded the emotions?

What was the situation?

_____

_____

What were your physical symptoms?

_____

_____

What were your thinking patterns?

_____

_____

What were your emotions?

_____

_____

When you are able to recall the emotions clearly, choose one of the following colours – green, blue, brown, black, yellow, orange, pink or white. **Draw** the emotion in colour on a clean sheet of paper. You may draw different aspects of the emotion, e.g. a snowman if the feeling is cold, or yourself behind bars if you feel trapped. Different symbols may be used to represent the emotions. (Alternative: Use the same colour clay and form the emotion in clay.)

**Note:** You may use this activity to process a traumatic event and to let go of it.

When you take information in through your senses, a few processes take place in your brain. Let us look at this in more detail.

"The biggest discovery of my generation is that people can change their life by changing their thoughts."
*William James*

## THE INTERPRETATION OF INFORMATION PERCEIVED BY THE SENSES

All human experiences are subjective, which means that no two persons will perceive and interpret the same situation or event in the same way. People can change their experiences by changing their feelings and thoughts about them, in other words the way in which they make an interpretation. Even deep-seated fears and habits can be overcome by thinking differently about them. The first big step you can take in terms of understanding interpretations is to realise that it can be different. What you think about something may not be correct and your "truth" may not be as true as you had thought! Another person's "truth" may also be true as it is according to his interpretation of the objective reality. Can you now see why misunderstandings happen so easily?

"Reality isn't the way you wish things to be, nor the way they appear to be, but the way they actually are."
*Robert J. Ringer*

### PERCEPTIONS
These are reactions to external events.

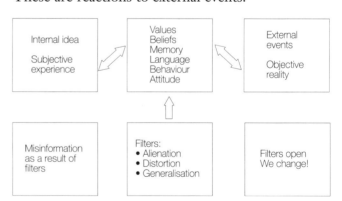

The objective reality perceived by a person is alienated, distorted or generalised by the person's filters which include aspects like his values, assumptions, attitudes, etc. (See the diagram above.) As a result of the filters, the person loses valuable information which could have made the "picture" of the objective reality more complete. Therefore he is drawing conclusions/making interpretations on incomplete data and thus has a subjective experience. The filters are working like a sieve, the holes of which are very small. Only that which the person wants to hear or experience is going through.

Examples of the functions of the filters are as follows:

- **Alienation:** This happens when a person has a certain experience but denies that it is applicable to him or that he has anything to do with it.
- **Distortion:** The information you receive is distorted to fit that which you are comfortable to accept. You see something as you would like to see it and not as it really is. If someone compliments you on your dress, you think that your hair/make-up/hands are not good enough to compliment.
- **Generalisation:** A certain event is generalised in terms of other events, e.g. your lover always brought you flowers when he cheated on you. Now you think that every time a man brings a woman flowers he has been untrue to her. You don't judge every event on its own merits. You may also think "everyone does it" or "nobody does it".

As soon as a person opens his filters (or uses a sieve with bigger holes!) he is able to see the whole picture – not as he would like to see it, but as it really is. To open your filters, you have to be prepared to look with "new" eyes at that which happens to others and yourself. You have to be prepared to question embedded values, etc. This also means that you have to take in all the information available about a certain situation before you come to a conclusion. For example: if one of your colleagues does not greet you at work one morning, you may immediately think that he does not like you. This interpretation will be easily made if you are feeling inferior. You will be upset and angry, with the result that you will ignore him for the rest of the day. If you had been prepared to gather more information about the situation you may have heard that he had had a bad day or that he was absent-minded. You could have decided not to be upset about it and to get more information about his mood later in the day. Always try to get as much information as possible about a situation before you make an interpretation. Things may be very different from what they seem at first!

"Things do not upset people. They become upset about how they see things."
*Marcus Aurelius*

## ACTIVITY 30: Are your perceptions objective?

As seen above, the interpretation of your perceptions is not necessarily correct. When you do this activity, you will see how easy it is to make the wrong interpretations. Do this activity with someone else. One of you tells something to the other one. The person listening has to show some nonverbal reaction. The first person who did the talking and the interpretation follows the next three steps:

1. Describe what you saw (the nonverbal reaction). ("While I was talking, you shook your head and rolled your eyes.")
2. Say what your interpretation of that reaction was. ("It appeared to me that you did not believe what I was saying.")
3. Verify – ask if your interpretation was correct or incorrect. ("Is it true?")

Always ensure as far as possible that what you think is going on is the reality by asking for confirmation. Develop your senses as fully as you can to be able to perceive all information.

In the following part we focus on the functioning of your brain, brain programmes and the importance of your brain profile in experiencing and processing of your emotions.

## THE FUNCTIONING OF THE BRAIN

New developments in neuro-biological data are giving us a better understanding of the brain. Human behaviour and the motivation for the behaviour can also be better explained. The brain is very powerful. It is your responsibility to gain as much information as possible about the functioning of your body and your brain in order to reach your potential. The more you use your brain, the more dendrites are formed between the neurones and the bigger your potential gets. Remember that each thought is essential to the formation of patterns in your brain. If you want to learn new behavioural patterns, you have to start thinking differently. In time your behaviour will change.

Keep in mind that water is an electrical impulse conductor, which improves the functioning of the brain. Drink at least eight glasses of water per day.

Your brain can simply be seen as two halves which function as a whole. The right side of your brain controls the left side of your body and the left side of your brain controls the right side of your body. The functions and parts of the brain are highly integrated; e.g. we use different parts of the brain to remember one situation (atmosphere, faces, events). It is a simplification to say that certain parts focus more on emotions, as the brain is much more integrated and complex than that. Damage to parts of the emotional brain harm the logical brain as well. The person will still be able to speak, but will have difficulty in making decisions, planning or building relationships. The rational and emotional parts of the brain are interdependent. Thus, emotional intelligence improves rational thinking and intellectual abilities as well.

The brain is roughly divided into three parts:

**Neocortex (higher brain):** This part of the brain is used for thinking, reasoning, memory, etc. Humans can think about the feelings they experience and can generate feelings by thinking about them. Your thoughts and feelings result in human behaviour.

**Limbic system:** This part of the brain is impulsive, powerful and emotional. It is focused on yourself. A two-year-old child functions to a large extent from this part. This can be identified by self-directed, emotional behaviour. Intense feelings like anxiety, frustration and anger can limit the functions of the neocortex, which means that the primitive brain takes charge. The implications of this are that logical reasoning is not possible and the person is not able to make well-considered decisions. This process can be explained as follows: all information coming from the senses is registered by the amygdala (part of the limbic system) before it goes to the neocortex. The functions of the brain can be "hijacked" by the amygdala in crisis situations, e.g. at a crime scene. Afterwards the person cannot remember what happened or why he did certain things.

**Reptile brain:** The human survival functions, impulses and reflexes are situated in the reptile brain. It is this part of the brain that protects you and enables you to act quickly when endangered. This is about fight or flight, pain or pleasure and expectations or reality. These survival functions are genetically transferred.

## Brain programmes

Your "consciousness" consists of three parts that are:

**Consciousness:** A person can only process a few pieces of new information at one time in the conscious part of his brain, e.g. remember a new address.

**Subconsciousness:** This information is readily available to you, e.g. information you knew well at some stage.

**Unconsciousness:** Most information, insights, etc. form part of your unconsciousness and are not always available to you. Your unconsciousness is much stronger than your consciousness. Negative thinking programmes your unconsciousness and has an influence on your behaviour. What you expose yourself to and how you want to programme yourself is your choice. Your brain cannot distinguish between positive and negative information or between imagination and reality. You should not only react to life, but take control and let good things happen.

Your memory is included in all three parts of your programmes. You can remember information which you processed recently, and information that you were familiar with in the past (which is in your subconscious). It is also possible to remember information that you have processed unconsciously, even though this information may only be retrieved with the help of hypnosis or therapy.

## The brain profile, dominances and their importance in terms of our relationships and emotions [11]

Paul E. Dennison (Ph.D.) did research on brain profiles and he formulated an explanatory or behavioural model. It is not a physiological-anatomical model. Its purpose is to provide a framework of the dominant parts of one's brain and senses as well as one's hands and feet. It explains how these dominances influence

one's functioning. Your profile influences the way in which you recognise, express and cope with your feelings, which means that people with different profiles will react differently to their emotions. The goal of this is the integration/balance between the functions of the different parts of the brain. It is the choice and responsibility of everyone to attain balance or to learn skills in order to cope with certain situations, e.g. communication with others (with the help of brain gym).

Although someone can learn new skills, he will tend to fall back on his genetic dominance. For example, a person who is gestalt (right brain) dominant and who is more emotional than a left brain dominant person can learn to think more logically about his problems. He may, however, experience problems controlling his emotions as soon he finds himself in a very stressful situation.

**BRAIN PROFILE**

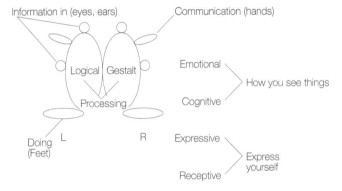

To understand the diagram above, consider the following: the two big ovals represent the big brain hemispheres where the processing of new information takes place. The two circles on top are the eyes while the two small circles at the sides are the ears. It is through these that information is taken in. The hands are close to the eyes and we communicate with them. The feet are at the bottom and they represent the doing/action of the person. The dominant one of each of these can be determined; in other words, the dominant eye, ear, foot, hand and brain hemisphere. In addition to this, it can be determined whether the person sees life from a cognitive (organised, logical, reserved) or an emotional (irrational, impulsive, feeling) perspective. Furthermore, it can be determined whether the person talks about his problems (is expressive) or quietly processes them inside himself (is receptive). Expressive people are action-oriented, active, proactive and interpersonal, while receptive people are mostly intrapersonal, thoughtful and passive. The dominances of a person are thus tested on three levels. It is preferable for a professional person (such as a qualified psychologist or therapist) to determine your dominances, as your seemingly dominant hand may not be genetically dominant, e.g. your right hand may be genetically dominant, but you may write with your left hand (functionally dominant).

A few of the characteristics of the dominances are as follows: (Remember that the right side of the brain controls the left side of your body and the other way around.)

**Hemispheres – processing of information:**
Left hemisphere (logic): the person controls his feelings and does not show them readily; sees detail; likes abstract ideas, reasoning, planning, facts, language; is a problem-solver, independent, auditive, visual, directed to the future, analytical, goal-orientated and objective.

Right hemisphere (gestalt): the person sees the whole picture, is sensitive, emotional, has insight, is able to visualise, is descriptive and creative, is adaptable, likes open ends, responds to movement, colour and pictures, is subjective, directed to the present rather than the future and is spontaneous.[12]

**Ears – receive information:**
Left ear dominant: listens to *how* someone says something, in other words the feeling behind the words and the meaning of it, the tone of the voice, etc.

Right ear dominant: listens to *what* is said (facts).

**Eyes – receive information:**
Left eye dominant: Wants to read from right to left and that may lead to reading problems. Sees what he wants to see and is not a credible eyewitness! Sees the whole of a situation and the meaning of it. Looks creatively at what could be.

Right eye dominant: Sees detail in a situation and may not get the big picture. Looks critically at what is there already (sees spelling errors easily).

**Feet – doing something:**
Left foot dominant: You tend to be impulsive, like variation and change.

Right foot dominant: Precise, controlled, constant, plan in detail before you do something. Hesitant.

**Hands – communication:**
Left hand dominant: emotional, likes touching, use your hands to complement your language.

Right hand dominant: precise, extended vocabulary, well spoken.

Different brain profiles explain the differences in human behaviour with regard to learning, taking action and reactions. **Knowing about this makes it more possible for you to have patience and empathy with other people, because you realise that people function differently and that they perceive their worlds differently.** What is important to one person (detail for the logical person) may not be important for the other person (gestalt). These differences may give rise to misunderstandings. A professional person who has been trained in this specifically can determine your brain profile. The testing is done by means of a physiological test ("muscle checking") and questions.[13]

## ACTIVITY 33: Eye dominance

To determine which eye is the dominant one, do the following activity. Hold your arms extended in front of you. Fold you hands over each other to form a triangle between your thumbs and index fingers so that you can look through them. Look through the opening with both eyes and focus on a mark or windowpane. First close your left eye while you look at the chosen "picture". Do the same with the other eye. The eye that sees the mark (the mark does not shift) is your dominant eye. When you look through the opening with your nondominant eye, the "picture" shifts and you see something else. You can control this by determining which eye stays open when you want to aim or wink. The one that stays open is your dominant eye.

## Ways in which emotions can be experienced and controlled

Your genetic brain dominance determines the way you experience and manage feelings.

Logic (left brain): the person tries harder and harder, looks mechanical and tense.

Gestalt (right brain): the person feels overwhelmed, does not remember detail and looks emotional.

Receptive: this person will feel better when he receives or does the following: supportive touching, exercising, visualising, listens to or plays music.

Expressive: the person will feel better when he receives or does the following: role-play, scream, cry, sigh, laugh, sing, draw, move.

## SUMMARY

You have come to the end of the first section about emotional awareness. At this stage you should know what feelings are, why they are important and where they come from. Remember that your values and assumptions play an important role in the way you look at and experience life. If you are still uncertain about the preceding section, read it once more. The better you understand and integrate it, the greater the possibility that change will take place. Take a breather and think about your new knowledge and skills.

In the next chapter we focus on the enhancement of your self-knowledge and the improvement of your self-acceptance. These aspects form the core of your humanity, from where you make choices and plan to function optimally. Thus it is the foundation for your own happiness and relationships with others.

# CHAPTER 3
## self-knowledge: who are you?

It is very important that you know and understand yourself in order to have a good relationship with yourself and others. Do you really know who you are and what you really want? When you know yourself, you know what is genuinely important to you and what your values and needs are. You know which aspects of yourself you are willing to make compromises about, and what you can't and don't want to change without giving up on yourself. The needs you are willing to make a compromise about are clear. You realise and enjoy the fact that you are unique, special and immeasurable.

## SELF-IMAGE?

Self-image is one of the aspects of humanity which has a big impact on people and about which a lot has been written. There are various definitions of self-image, but in short it means what you think about yourself. This picture which you have about yourself is primarily based on two sources: the feedback you receive from other people (especially those on whose opinion you rely a lot, e.g. your parents, spouse, etc.) and your behaviour or skills.

Self-image is often described as a feeling you have about yourself. However, it is not a feeling, but rather a measure of your own worth as a result of the two sources mentioned above, i.e. the feedback you receive from others and your skills. You have to put these two aspects in context in terms of the feedback you have received during your lifetime from all the different people you have had contact with and all the skills/behaviour you have shown during this time (acknowledging the consequences for yourself and other people). You will realise that the average person has contact with hundreds of other people and that you may have shown as many as 50 000 different kinds of conduct and skills. If you want to measure yourself to get an objective evaluation, you will need to measure all the feedback and all your skills at a certain time. This is however impossible, as others can only see a small part of you at a given time and because you can only remember a few details of what happened to you. Visualise a big circle with a much smaller circle in the middle.

The big circle shows the total feedback and skills, while the small circle represents the part that you can remember. Thus it is impossible for you to measure yourself with any kind of reliability.

If you consider the way a person thinks about and measures himself, it is clear that this is not the right way to go about it. Instead of measuring the feedback that you receive in terms of a specific situation, you measure your whole person against it.

We will try to explain it in a practical way. Your husband/wife/significant other tells you that you do not look good in your new outfit or that he/she wants to break up the relationship with you. What is your immediate reaction? Yes, you overreact instead of seeing it in context – as a single example of negative feedback. You measure your total persona against that and immediately see yourself as worthless. What would you have thought if the same thing had happened to your best friend? You would have seen it more in context and you would have realised that her self-worth should have stayed the same. You can't use a single event to measure your worth and you should stay objective so that it can be put in perspective. You are worth much more than a single skill or a single piece of negative feedback (which may not even be valid). It makes no sense to think that you are worth nothing just because you are not good at cooking or baking or playing golf. What about everything else you can do?[14]

## MASKS

Most people wear a mask some time during their lives. The purpose of it is, *inter alia*, to hide something from others or to pretend to be something that you are not. It takes a great deal of energy to wear a mask and not be yourself. You can use this energy much more meaningfully by disclosing yourself and building relationships with the knowledge that others accept you as you are. Sometimes, however, it may be necessary to wear a mask – but you have to determine the price you will pay.[15] Do Activity 34 on masks (next three pages) to become aware of what you hide from and show to people. This may help to improve your self-knowledge.

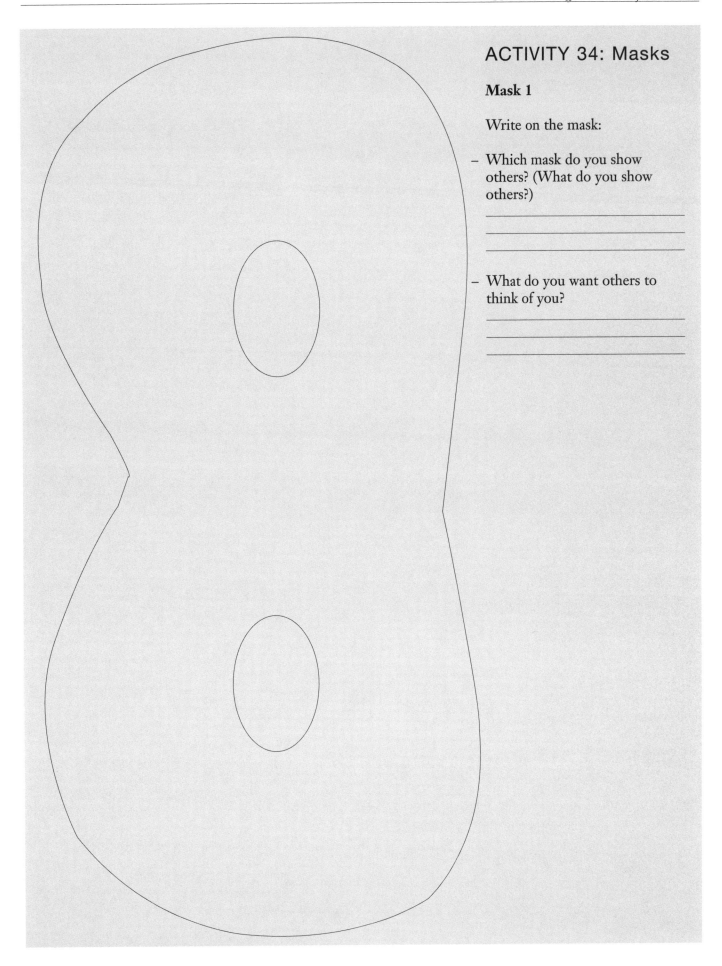

## ACTIVITY 34: Masks

**Mask 1**

Write on the mask:

– Which mask do you show others? (What do you show others?)

_____
_____
_____


– What do you want others to think of you?

_____
_____
_____

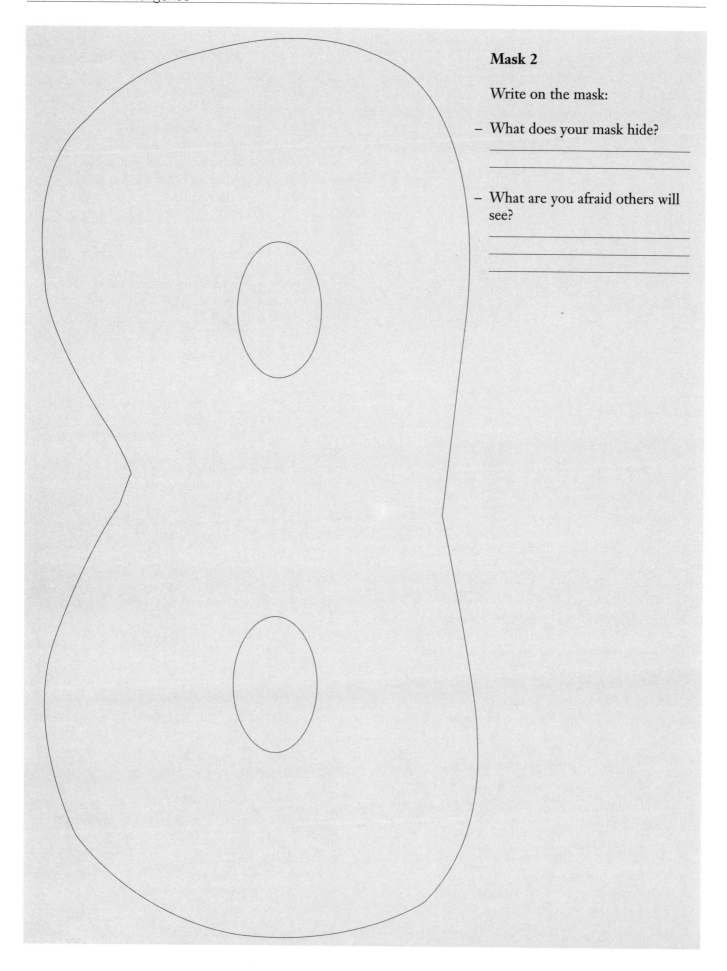

## Mask 2

Write on the mask:

– What does your mask hide?

_____

_____

– What are you afraid others will
see?

_____

_____

_____

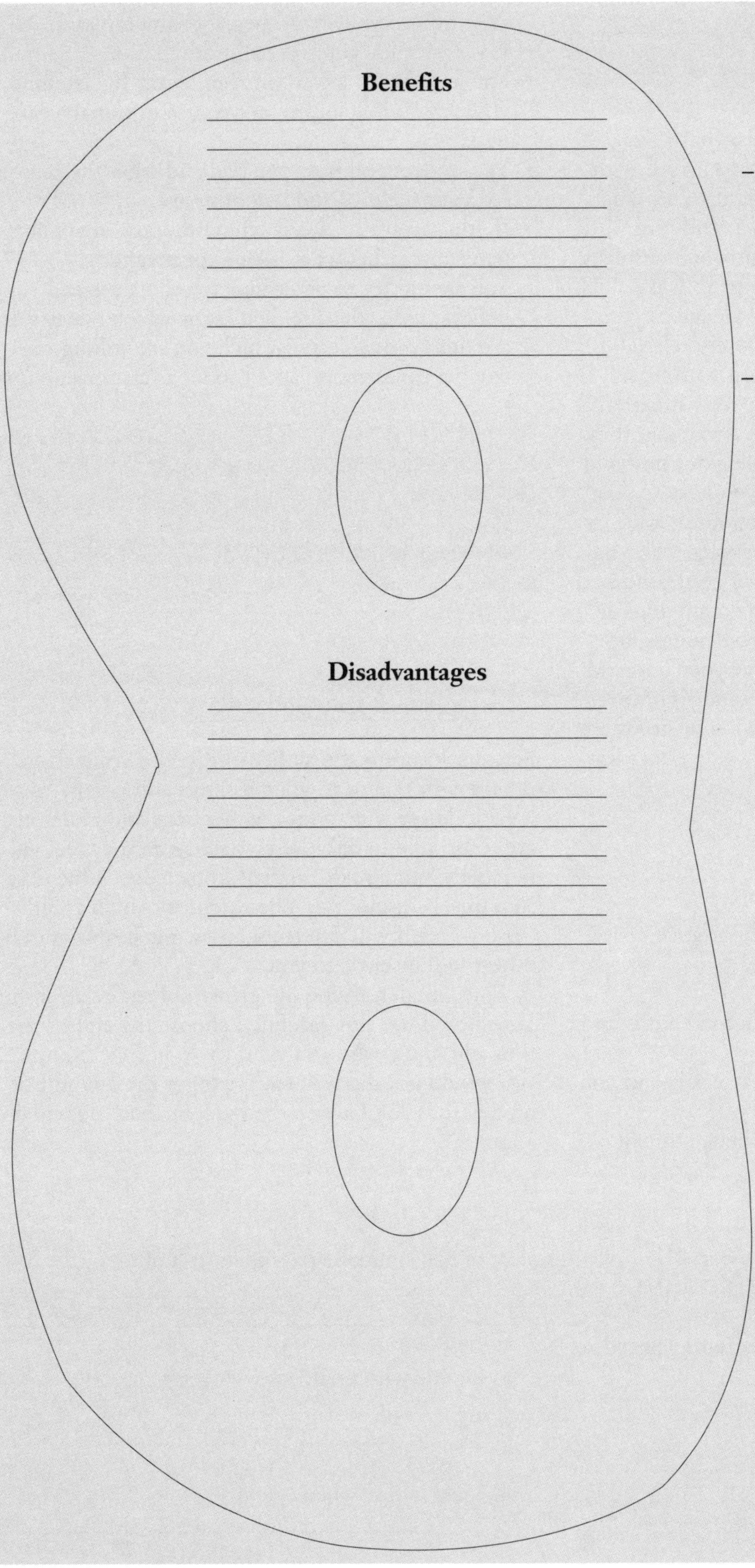

**Benefits**

_____
_____
_____
_____
_____
_____
_____
_____
_____

**Disadvantages**

_____
_____
_____
_____
_____
_____
_____
_____
_____
_____

**Mask 3**

Write on the mask:

– What are the benefits for you
  and others when you wear a
  mask?

_____
_____
_____

– What are the disadvantages for
  you and others when you wear a
  mask?

_____
_____
_____

## THE IMPORTANCE OF SELF-KNOWLEDGE

Ask yourself the following question: is what I am telling myself the truth, or am I lying to myself without being aware of it? Is this how I want to be, what other people expect me to be or how I really am? One frequently deceives oneself about who one really is and what one's intentions are. The truth is usually something which is difficult to acknowledge to yourself and difficult to change. This is closely related to denial and blaming. When I am honest with myself I accept responsibility for changing my own situation. I don't expect others to behave in such a way that they fulfil my needs. Consider this example: your husband is working late and you believe that you have to wait up for him. While you are waiting you don't want to do anything so that you will be unoccupied when he arrives. You start blaming him for your restlessness, while you are not really motivated to do anything in the meantime. The reason for your restlessness lies within yourself, but you want to blame your husband for it. The question is: are you being totally honest with yourself, about who you are, what your needs are and where you are heading? The following quotation is applicable to this. Remember it!

"Am I telling myself the truth?"
*Anonymous*

The following factors confirm the importance of self-knowledge:

* If you know yourself, you know your strengths and growth areas.
* You are able to accept yourself more easily and you can fulfil your potential.
* You do not compare yourself to others, but pay attention to your own special characteristics.
* It is easier for you to accept others.
* You are able to know yourself better by listening to yourself and by improving your emotional awareness.
* You understand how you feel and what the reasons for your feelings and reactions are.
* If you receive feedback from others, you are able to determine whether it is valid or invalid.
* You should try to determine which values and beliefs guide your life. You know which needs/values are nonnegotiable and which you are willing to reach a compromise about to let a relationship grow.

"When you go up to meet your Creator, He only asks one question: Were you you?"
*Leo Buscaglia*

"It is never too late to be what you might have been."
*George Eliot*

## SELF-DISCLOSURE

Self-disclosure is the ability to disclose yourself to others with regard to your feelings and needs. You have to know what your own feelings and reactions are to be able to disclose yourself. You may feel vulnerable when you do so. Self-knowledge is the first step in self-disclosure. The extent to which you disclose yourself will determine how much of themselves others will disclose to you.

This will determine the growth of the relationship. You should use this carefully: choose the right situation and know why you want to do it. For example: you would not disclose to a stranger the amount of money that you have in the bank or that you had an affair!

### ACTIVITY 35: To improve self-knowledge and self-disclosure

**A. Complete the following statements regarding yourself:**

1. People who like me
_____
_____

2. When someone pays me a compliment, I
_____
_____

3. People who really know me say
_____
_____

4. I feel happy when
_____

5. I like people who

_____

_____

6. I am

_____

_____

7. If someone confronts me, I

_____

_____

8. I feel hurt when

_____

_____

9. Few people know that I

_____

_____

10. Right now, I feel (an emotion)

_____

_____

because (the reason)

_____

_____

**B. Answer the following questions on a separate sheet of paper.**

1. When and where do you feel most relaxed?

2. What are the four most important things in your life? Say why.

3. How do you feel about yourself most of the time?

4. Name two people who have supported you in your life.

5. Have you ever felt that your heart is broken? When?

6. What do you like most in yourself – your appearance, your personality or your intellect?

7. If you could relive one year of your life, which year would it be and why?

8. What was a turning point in your life?

9. What encourages you to cope with life?

10. How do you decide between right and wrong?

11. Which important lesson in life have you learnt already?

12. How do you feel when you are at home alone? What do you do then?

13. What are your goals and ideals and why?

14. What do you think of when you think about your childhood?

15. What do you think about when you can't sleep?

16. Who can console you?

17. What aspect of yourself would you want people to remember?

18. What would you do if you knew that you would die soon?

19. What (have you realised lately) would ensure that you enjoy life more?

20. What impact does stress have on your life?

21. What are your hopes and fears for the future?

22. Whom would you borrow money from in case of need?

23. Whom would you phone first if you experienced a crisis?

24. In which ways are you like your parents? How do you feel about that?

25. How do you feel if someone criticises you?

26. Have you ever felt guilty? Why?

27. How do you feel about homelessness, poverty, child abuse, disability, etc.?

28. If you could make a law to guide people's lives, what would it be?

29. What does nobody know about you?

30. When do you experience feelings of hurt?

31. When do you get frustrated, sad, depressed, angry, etc.?

32. What do you believe in?

33. What in yourself do you dislike?

34. What do you want your last words to be?

35. When do you feel embarrassed and how do you react then?

36. What would you never do/never forget?

37. What age would you like to be? Why?

38. What in yourself do you like especially?

39. What are you thankful for?

40. What would make your life easier?

41. How do you react when something does not work out as planned?

42. What do you feel if you look in the mirror?

43. When do you feel happy and satisfied?

44. What makes you happy?

45. What does happiness mean to you?

46. If it were possible for you to acquire another talent/skill, what would it be?

47. If you had had more time, what would you have done?

48. What should you have done a long time ago?

49. What do you neglect?

50. What would you like to do once again?

51. What would you like to do before the end of the year?

52. What do you think about when you are alone?

53. What are your three biggest wishes?

54. What is your greatest fear?

55. If everything were taken away from you, what three things would you like to keep?

56. What do you feel sometimes?

57. What do you feel when you think about your life?

58. What is the one thing that you would want to rescue if your house were on fire?

59. What was your dream as a child?

60. What motivates you from day to day?

61. What is your favourite colour?

62. Where in nature do you find rest for your soul?

63. To which kind of music do you like to listen?

64. What would you do if you were rich?

65. What do you wish you could change?

66. Who are you?

67. What do you think about every day?

68. What is a "hot button" for you? (When do you get angry?)

69. What is a "cold button" for you? (When do you take time out?)

70. What characteristic in you is disliked most by others?

71. Describe the person you want to be.

72. Which of your dreams have you not realised?

73. Draw up a list of activities that make you successful. Evaluate how many are cognitive and how many are emotional.

**C. See yourself as a tree and then answer the following questions:**

1. What kind of tree are you?
_____
_____

2. Are you deciduous or not?
_____
_____

3. Do you have fruit or flowers or both?
_____
_____

4. What are your branches and leaves like?
_____
_____

5. Do you have to be pruned?
_____
_____

6. Have you been pruned already?
_____
_____

7. What kind of root system do you have?
_____
_____

8. How often do you need water, sun and fertiliser?
_____
_____

9. Do you have birds nesting in your branches?
_____
_____

10. Do you have insects in your bark, which are destroying you?
_____
_____

11. Are your leaves, fruit or flowers poisonous?
_____
_____

12. Do you have thorns?
_____
_____

13. What is your function? (Do you provide shade or are you a fruit tree?)
_____
_____

Read your answers carefully. What do they say about you? Are you satisfied with yourself or do you want to change certain things? Change those things that you can. Which are truly part of you? Which are nonnegotiable and which are the things you are prepared to reach a compromise about?

Temperament tests like the Keirsey-Bates and Myers-Briggs may give you valuable information about certain dominances or tendencies in yourself in terms of thoughts, reactions and feelings. This will improve your self-knowledge.[16]

## ACTIVITY 36: Improve your self-knowledge

If a stranger looks at the contents of your handbag/briefcase/desk drawer what will he/she learn about you?

"You are the captain of your ship. Who has the rudder?"
*Anonymous*

## SELF-ACCEPTANCE

The first and most important step anyone can take in his life is to accept himself and those around him unconditionally. You may decide to accept yourself as you are without changing anything or you may decide to learn certain skills in order to grow and develop. The decision about this rests within yourself, as only you are able to change yourself. How important is it to you to change? There are certain aspects which you will not be able to change and that you will have to accept without continually struggling to change them. Let them go and use the energy for something that you are able to change. If you accept yourself, you have confidence in yourself and in your abilities. Win or lose, you believe that you are a worthy person.

People who accept themselves feel good about themselves and are more effective and productive. They are proud of what they have achieved and they usually don't compare it with the achievements of others. It is possible for them to enjoy life and they trust themselves.

These people can perform independently, are able to make well-considered decisions and take responsibility, and they are successful in their jobs and personal relationships. It is not necessary for them to receive the approval of others to feel good about themselves. People who accept themselves can take risks, accept their mistakes and assert themselves in various situations. They leave the past behind and strive to reach their goals.

The greatest contribution you can make to any relationship is to love and accept yourself, as what you believe about yourself is projected onto your relationships. For example, if you believe that you are an easy person to be with, it will be easy for other people to be involved with you.

If you believe in and accept yourself, you have gained a very important victory. You are unique and valuable. Accept what you are and choose to change what you want to change. You may be yourself and you may make mistakes.

When you accept the things you cannot change, you have the energy to change what you are able to. Don't give up too easily when trying to change things. If you always see your accomplishments as "not good enough", they will feel that way to you, irrespective of other people's opinion of them.

"Judgement is more than a habit, it is a way of life. Your judgements stain the windows of your perception (filters). They filter everything you see so that, in truth, you see nothing as it really is; you see only your judgements. Thus, you do not see your own beauty, wholeness and Light within, you see only that you 'could do better' and 'could be more'."
*Robert Holden*

**Tips to become more self-accepting:**
- Accept and make peace with yourself – physically and emotionally. Have realistic expectations of yourself.
- Don't compare yourself to others. If you compare yourself to others who have more skills or wealth than yourself, you will experience negative feelings. When you compare yourself to those who have less than you do, you will experience ambivalent feelings, since you think you ought to feel good. That may not be the way you really feel. You are unique! Remember that you are immeasurable.
- Focus on your strengths and positive traits and try to improve your growth areas.
- Be responsible for your own happiness and feelings. Choose consciously to be happy.
- Take risks and be prepared to make mistakes. A person's level of EI is mirrored in his willingness to learn from his mistakes. Be persistent. Don't try to be perfect and don't expect perfection from others.

### ACTIVITY 37: Advertise yourself

The purpose of this activity is to enable you to recognise your positive traits and to describe them. Thus, it is to enhance your self-esteem. Imagine that you have to make a presentation of yourself to a firm who may be interested in employing you. You have to be honest. The art will be in presenting the truth in its most positive light. Draw a logo for yourself and think of any additional materials that you could include in your presentation, such as photos, certificates, and references from other people. Write the presentation in about ten sentences. Do it on a coloured piece of paper and get it laminated.

"Don't compromise yourself – you are all you've got."
*Janis Joplin*

## SELF-ASSERTIVENESS

Self-assertiveness means to have self-confidence about what you want and to be able to communicate effectively about it. It does not mean that you will always get your own way. You should be able to com-promise. For example, you are able to ask if you can postpone a task you are given until the next day, as you already have an appointment. It is self-affirmative behaviour that proves to you that you are worthwhile and valuable. It confirms your beliefs as to who you are and what you want from other people. You are

## ACTIVITY 38: Four styles of behaviour/communication

| | STYLE OF BEHAVIOUR | Think of an example (any role or situation) where you use or have used one of these styles. Write it down here. |
|---|---|---|
| X | **Passive**<br>*You express your feelings indirectly.<br>*You avoid conflict.<br>*You find it difficult to say "no".<br>*You feel hopeless.<br>*Your needs are not fulfilled.<br>*Your pain accumulates.<br>*You blame others.<br>*You feel invisible.<br>*Others have to guess your needs. | |
| X | **Aggressive**<br>*You have the impulse to punish.<br>*People avoid you.<br>*You experience conflict with others.<br>*You want to be in control.<br>*You want others to accept your opinion.<br>*You are overwhelming.<br>*You blame others. | |
| X | **Manipulative**<br>*You use dramatic silences.<br>*You are overenthusiastic.<br>*You want sympathy.<br>*You consciously lower your voice.<br>*You focus on certain words to persuade others.<br>*You may touch the other person unnecessarily and inappropriately.<br>*You may use dramatic gestures. | |
| ✓ | **Self-assertive behaviour**<br>*You verbalise facts and are honest.<br>*You diminish anger.<br>*You stand by your rights.<br>*You look for a solution.<br>*You set limits.<br>*People respect you.<br>*You care about yourself and others. | |

able to say: "I prefer . . . " rather than "I have to . . ."

Self-assertiveness means that you have respect for the right of others to assert themselves as well. When you decide to keep quiet in certain situations, you are asserting yourself. If you are self-assertive you are able to cope with most situations with ease. You realise that your own needs and wishes are different from those of others. You let yourself make mistakes and acknowledge them, but you know how to recognise and enjoy your successes as well.

Becoming self-assertive is a process that calls for self-awareness and practice. You have to be on the lookout for situations in which you can assert yourself. You can learn a lot from seeing how other people assert themselves. Self-acceptance enables you to assert yourself, while heightened self-assertiveness may improve your self-acceptance, because you are getting to feel better about yourself.

You usually show one of four types of behaviour: aggressive, passive, manipulative or self-assertive.[17] Activity 38 expounds on these behaviours and helps you to determine which type of behaviour is applicable to you. You may behave differently in different situations.

## How to express yourself effectively, self-assertively:

Use the following guidelines to be more self-assertive:
- Validate the feelings of the other person. (This is discussed in more detail in the next chapter.)
- Put forward your position with self-confidence.
- Say "no" if you mean "no".
- Take your time.
- Don't say you are sorry or make excuses.
- Don't let yourself or others feel inferior.
- Be specific.
- Be aware of your voice and body language. Maintain eye contact.
- Don't feel guilty if you want to say "no".
- Cope with the criticism that you may receive.

## Why do I say "yes" when I want to say "no" ?

The following are possible situations in which you may find yourself and in which you may find it difficult to say "no".
- Are you afraid of the consequences if you say "no"? Will someone use it against you? Will it be repeated to others?
- You may see it as part of your role, e.g. in family matters. It is very difficult to say "no" to family members.
- You are afraid of rejection, as you base your worthiness on your actions. You feel good if you say "yes" and please others.
- You want to be seen in a positive light.
- You feel indebted to someone. This overwhelms you and it "forces" you to say "yes".

What are your values and assumptions? What you believe in may be hampering your self-assertiveness, as you may believe that it is bad manners to say "no"!

## How to say "no"

Refuse self-assertively as clearly and as persistently as you can and without aggression. You have the right to say "no". Use your sixth sense and ask for time to think about the request. Don't do anything out of pity if it leaves you feeling misused or unwilling. Acknowledge your feelings: "I have helped you often with this lately. I feel misused."

Change the subject after you have said "no"; if you don't you will give the other person the opportunity to question you or force you to do something you don't want to do. You don't have to explain why you don't want to do something. Use the same words as the other person: "Do you want to buy this product?" "No, I don't want to buy this product." You may say "no" and give an alternative: "I cannot work overtime tonight, but it will be possible tomorrow night." Your body language is very important. Maintain eye contact, stand up straight, not too far from or too close to the other person; your nonverbal communication has to radiate self-confidence. Be calm, don't frown, speak clearly and at a comfortable rhythm. Don't sigh, clench your fists, narrow your eyes or be too friendly. Remember that asserting yourself is a choice and you have to believe so much in what you say that you are willing to bear the consequences.

## Setting boundaries

Boundaries define for us who we are; where we begin and where we end. They give us a feeling of ownership and responsibility for our life. One should set external boundaries, which show other people where they stand. Your internal boundaries help you to say "no" to destructive needs and to delay the satisfaction of certain needs. You should also determine which kinds of thoughts you are going to allow yourself. It is important to communicate your boundaries to all those you are in a relationship with, because it brings security and openness to a relationship. When you experience feelings of disgust, frustration or anger when people don't respect you, you have to set new boundaries or communicate them more clearly. Ask yourself: do I have the right to get angry when others take control of my life? Take responsibility for and control your life and move purposefully in the direction of the goals you have set for yourself.

## ACTIVITY 39: Self-assertiveness

This activity evaluates your skill at asserting yourself. Imagine the following situations. You must assert yourself and keep your viewpoint. Ask someone to help you if this is something you really have to practise.

1. You have just won R100 000 in a competition. You have already decided what you want to do with the money. A few people from a welfare organisation try to persuade you to give most of the money to them. Assert yourself and refuse to give them any of the money.

2. Your boss asks you to work overtime at the weekend to finish an important project. You have already worked two weekends this month and you have an appointment with some friends on Saturday. Try to reach a compromise.

3. You are working on a special project that is nearly finished. You are enjoying it and have everything organised in order to compile a well-researched report. Your boss wants you to put that aside in favour of a more urgent project. Assert yourself and say that you want to finish your first project before starting the next.

4. You bought a radio from someone and later you find that it is not working. The person involved refuses to replace or repair it. Assert yourself in this situation.

5. Your mother is arranging a family gathering for a weekend you want to go camping. Your reservations have been made already and your friends will be joining you. Assert yourself and refuse to go to the family gathering.

Complete the following sentences to identify the situations in which you find it difficult to assert yourself.

## ACTIVITY 40: The art of self-assertiveness and saying "no"

1. It is difficult for me to say "no" to

_____

_____

2. It is difficult for me to say "no" to

_____

_____

3. It is difficult for me to say "no" to

_____

_____

4. It is difficult for me to say "no" to

_____

_____

5. It is difficult for me to say "no" to

_____

_____

With regard to your new knowledge, how will you now assert yourself? Choose two of the situations described above and write down what you would say.

1. _____

_____

_____

2. _____

_____

_____

The following philosophy gives you the courage to assert yourself. Make a copy of this and put it where you can frequently read it.

## A SELF-ASSERTIVE PHILOSOPHY

1. By standing up for my rights I show respect to myself and I will probably also receive it from others.

2. By trying to avoid hurting other people I eventually hurt others as well as myself.

3. By sacrificing my rights, relationships are often broken and new ones are prevented from developing.

4. It is a form of selfishness to exclude others from my thoughts and feelings.

5. Sacrificing my rights teaches others to disregard me.

6. If I fail to notify others how their behaviour negatively affects me, I fail to give them the opportunity to change their behaviour.

7. I can decide what is important to me; it is not necessary for me to suffer under the tyranny of "must".

8. I appreciate myself more if I do what I believe is right and it improves my relationships with others.

9. I can insist on courtesy and respect.

10. I have the right to express myself in any way as long as I do not infringe upon the rights of others.

11. I have the right to keep quiet.

12. I do not need to please everyone all the time.

13. I have the right to know what is going on.

14. I do not need to give explanations for everything.

15. I do not need to feel guilty if I say "no" or if I put myself first.

16. I am not responsible for the other people's problems.

17. I have the right to express my opinion and negotiate for change.

18. I have the right to be listened to.

19. I have the right to make decisions and bear the consequences of my choices responsibly.[18]

## CHOICES AND RESPONSIBILITIES

Look at your life and consider the following question carefully: Does your present lifestyle bring you closer to your goals and does it embrace your values? If not, why not? Do you know what it is you want to expose yourself to? The answers may bring you closer to well-considered choices. Continually focus on what you can do and not on what you can't do. What in your life is keeping you from growing and in what can you put your trust? When you have to make

---

### ACTIVITY 41: What price do I pay?*

What price have I paid (or do I still pay) for poor self-acceptance, a lack of confidence, self-assertiveness and/or poorly defined boundaries?

1. At work:
_____
_____

2. With friends:
_____
_____

3. In my love life:
_____
_____

4. In my education/choice of career:
_____
_____

important decisions, always take the positive, constructive option rather than the destructive option. You have to change because you want to and not because it is expected of you. If you really want to change, it will be easier for you, as the motivation will come from yourself.

Remember that no one controls your actions or thoughts – you are in control of them. It is correct to say: "I am getting angry . . ." rather than "You are making me angry . . ." You have the freedom to choose how you want to feel and how you want to behave within certain rules of acceptable behaviour (e.g. the laws of a country). Even when your choices are limited, you still have choices. Sometimes you have to make a difficult choice from a few difficult alternatives. How do you decide between two equally difficult alternatives? It is important always to give yourself three alternatives from which you have to choose. This gives you more room to make a choice and it removes the "right or wrong" issue. When you have to decide about something, ask yourself the following: am I choosing this alternative because I really believe it is right or because I am afraid of the consequences should I choose the other alternative? This has to do with your motivation for choosing a certain alternative. Remember that not making a choice is a choice as well. To ponder on different choices uses a lot of emotional energy. Making a decision provides energy for action.

Having too rigid ideas about something may limit your choices, e.g. "A mother's task is to . . ." or "Men are like that . . ." These irrational assumptions may be detrimental to your decision-making. You can't dodge your responsibilities – each choice you make involves certain responsibilities that you have to accept. You are the result of the choices you have made and are making. Even if you are asserting yourself, you are still responsible for your behaviour and actions towards others. Self-assertiveness does not imply insensitivity or noninvolvement. To take responsibility is to decide what you want from life and then to strive for it. *Only you can live your own life.* Start to think about what you can do for yourself and not what others can do for you. Your choice can be positive in terms of a challenge or it may be negative and a threat. If you choose to see life as a challenge, there is hope, forgiveness, health, etc. If not, despair, stress and illness may be yours.

Impulsiveness or the immediate satisfaction of needs frequently brings no lasting happiness. In order to control impulsiveness, you have to formulate clear, attainable goals and often remind yourself of them. Visualise your goals and your feelings when you have achieved them. Think about what you stand to lose if you give in to your impulsiveness. Be aware of your real needs and don't try to fill your inner emptiness with impulsive behaviour. Assert yourself by saying "no" when you do not need temporary satisfaction of your needs.

Use the robot technique to control your feelings and to gain clear thinking. (This and other techniques are discussed in Chapter 5.) Impulsiveness is not always negative. You have to maintain a balance. If you are a very rigid, cautious person, you may benefit by an impulsive decision to do something enjoyable.

"One's philosophy is not expressed in words but in the choices one makes – and these choices are eventually one's own responsibility."
*Eleanor Roosevelt*

## BALANCE

Everyone is responsible for planning his life so that it is in balance and he can reach his full potential in each area of his life. We frequently focus only on our work or home to the exclusion of other important parts of our humanity. One of the most important aspects of an emotionally intelligent person is his ability to manage his lifestyle. This implies that you are able to keep a balance between all the facets of your life, i.e. physical, psychological/emotional, spiritual, intellectual and social. The balance may differ from person to person, but it is essential for self-actualisation. If you do not have balance, symptoms may arise which indicate unfulfilled needs. Unpleasant or negative feelings may be experienced. Have a look at the following activity. Evaluate to what extent you spend time in terms of your values and different parts of yourself, and whether your choices are in accordance with what you believe in. If knowledge is a very important value to you, how much time do you spend giving attention to it and gaining more of it?

# ACTIVITY 42: Activity analysis

Days and time spent in terms of hours per activity. Try to divide every hour of your day into one of the categories.

| Activity | Mon | Tues | Wednes | Thurs | Fri | Sat | Sun |
|---|---|---|---|---|---|---|---|
| PHYSICAL<br>Rest (sleep, snooze) | | | | | | | |
| Exercise | | | | | | | |
| Diet (content and method) | | | | | | | |
| Relaxation (meditating, music, art, reading, etc.) | | | | | | | |
| Sexual/sensual | | | | | | | |
| WORK/CAREER/HOUSE-HOLD TASKS, E.G. CHILDREN | | | | | | | |
| INTELLECTUAL<br>Planning/decisions | | | | | | | |
| Training/personal growth | | | | | | | |
| Goals/time management | | | | | | | |
| PSYCHOLOGICAL/EMOTIONAL<br>Self-awareness/withdrawal | | | | | | | |
| Self-knowledge/analysis | | | | | | | |
| Feelings | | | | | | | |
| SOCIAL<br>Support systems | | | | | | | |
| Friends/family | | | | | | | |
| Community involvement | | | | | | | |
| Cultural | | | | | | | |
| SPIRITUAL/RELIGIOUS<br>Involvement | | | | | | | |
| | | | | | | | |

| Activity | Mon | Tues | Wednes | Thurs | Fri | Sat | Sun |
|---|---|---|---|---|---|---|---|
| Goal and meaning | | | | | | | |
| OTHER | | | | | | | |

After you have completed the above, indicate with a * the activities which you especially enjoy. Plan to make them part of your daily lifestyle. If you find it difficult to do this, plan two activities in your journal. Some are pleasurable activities like having a picnic, going to the movies or visiting someone. Some of the other activities are work, such as working at the computer, attending meetings or preparing meals. Plan so that you have daily activities of both types. This will give you something to look forward to while you do the less pleasurable activities as well.

Now do Activity 43: Courses of action to achieve balance on p. 86.

## HOW MUCH TIME DO YOU SPEND ON YOURSELF?[19]

It is important that we spend a certain amount of time on ourselves, in order to relax, grow and learn more about ourselves. Most people say that they spend the minimum amount of time on themselves, or that they are even afraid of being alone.

You can do things with other people, as long as they are enjoyable and relaxing, like exercising, working in the garden, etc. It is also important to do things on your own, like reading or listening to music. A lot of people find it difficult to be alone and not do anything in particular, like sitting in the garden. The most difficult thing is to be alone **in silence** and not do anything. You could then meditate, pray or just relax. The following activity is valuable in making you aware of how little time you may spend on yourself, and perhaps it will motivate you to give yourself more attention.

## ACTIVITY 44: Analysis of time devoted to yourself

Indicate what you did and for how long.

| Activity | Relaxation with others | Not with others – – did something | Not with others – did nothing | Alone – silence – did nothing |
|---|---|---|---|---|
| Mon | | | | |
| Tues | | | | |
| Wednes | | | | |
| Thurs | | | | |
| Fri | | | | |
| Sat | | | | |
| Sun | | | | |

# ACTIVITY 43: Courses of action to achieve balance

Indicate in the small columns whether the activity has to be done daily (d), weekly (w) or monthly (m).

| Physical | | Spiritual/religious | | Emotional/psychological | | Social | | Intellectual | |
|---|---|---|---|---|---|---|---|---|---|
| **Exercise:** Walking, stretching, aerobic exercises. | | Purpose and meaning of life. | | Intrapersonal skills: Catharsis, self-knowledge, self-awareness, emotional control, acceptance, humour. | | Interpersonal skills: Listening, self-assertiveness, self-disclosure, facilitative questions, positive reforming, empathy, validation, restore relationships, forgiveness. Give attention to your social support systems. | | Thoughts and perceptions, assumptions, personal values and needs, rationalisations. Channel your thoughts, attitudes, change, positive reframing. | |
| **Diet:** 15% protein, 30% fat, 55% combined carbohydrates, potassium, B vitamins + micronutrients. Eat slowly, regularly, small portions. Exclude sodium (salt), alcohol and caffeine. Drink 6-8 glasses water per day. Eat fresh fruit, vegetables (dark green leaves), fish, nuts and fibre. | | – Why am I here? – What is my task regarding others and myself? – Related to your mission (see p. 132). | | | | | | | |
| **Relaxation:** Exercise, progressive muscle relaxation, imagination, deep breathing, massage, yoga, meditation. | | | | | | **Personal coping:** eliminate circumstances that cause the problem, keep consequences within manageable boundaries, (direct/ indirect, active/inactive). | | **Accept** responsibility for your own life. Visualisation. Realistic goals, lifestyle management, training, planning, time management, decision-making. | |
| Aromatherapy reduces stress as sense of smell is directly connected to "emotional brain". | | | | | | | | | |
| **Activities:** Follow up medical problems, maintain a healthy lifestyle, slow down your pace, become involved in sport, music or art, control your weight. | | | | | | | | | |
| **Rest:** 7-8 hours of sleep, snooze (20 minutes). Don't sleep in front of television, telephone or cellphone because of electromagnetic fields. | | | | | | | | | |
| **Natural light:** Receive enough natural light daily – it does not have to be direct sunlight. | | | | | | | | | |
| **Colour:** Blue and green are important regarding optimal brain functioning. Spend time in nature. Surround yourself with natural materials like wood and cane. | | | | | | | | | |
| **Physical touch:** Hugs and touching. Acknowledge the importance of sensual and sexual needs in yourself. | | | | | | | | | |

Now return to p. 85.

## SUMMARY

The goal of this chapter is mainly to guide you to more self-knowledge. However, it will also assist you to know and express your own needs and wishes, especially in situations where you have to assert yourself. Emphasis is given to the importance of self-acceptance and the improvement of those traits where growth is possible. Ensure that you make well-considered choices and take responsibility for them. At the end of the chapter, attention is given to the importance of balance in your life.

We have now reached the end of the first three parts where the emphasis is on you. You have given attention to your emotional awareness and improved your self-knowledge. These two components form the intrapersonal intelligence mentioned at the beginning of the book. In the following chapters we focus on communication with the people around you and coping with emotions and situations where other people are involved. Knowledge of and skills in this are essential because it is such an important part of healthy relationships. This is the interpersonal intelligence which forms part of EI.

# CHAPTER 4
## communication skills

The interaction between people is a complex process, which is made up of various interwoven aspects. We cannot discuss all of these aspects and will only pay attention to the most important ones. It is very important for everyone to have good, effective communication skills, because we are social beings who interact constantly with each other. In this chapter we discuss the most important aspects of communication, as they are applicable to the emotionally effective person.

## COMPONENTS OF COMMUNICATION

Communication consists of verbal and nonverbal messages which are exchanged between people. As people frequently do not have good communication skills and their perceptions are different, these messages can easily be misunderstood. There are several components of communication that you need to consider.

**What is communication?**

The exchange of messages between people

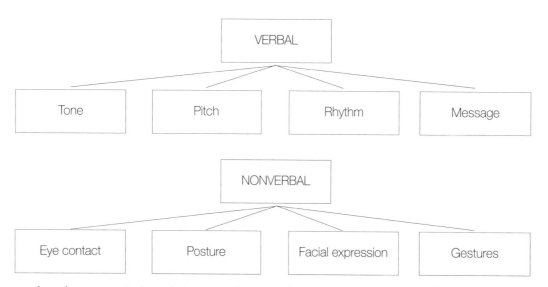

It is important that the tone, pitch and rhythm of your voice are consistent with the verbal message. Don't say in a high-pitched voice: "I am not mad at you!" Remember that your body language, like your facial expression, says a lot about how you really feel.

Both the sender (the one who speaks) and the receiver (the one who listens) have certain responsibilities:

**Sender:**
Is my message clear?
Do I have the receiver's attention?
What is my body language saying?
Do I know who the receiver is?

**Receiver:**
Do I understand the message correctly?
Am I giving my full attention to the sender?
Are the verbal and nonverbal messages the same?
Am I listening with empathy?

Communication is the foundation of all relationships – different roles mean different ways of communicating. Be careful not to talk to your spouse in the same way as you do to your children. Effective communication means that the receiver receives the message as the sender intended it to be. Misunderstandings occur as a result of differences in perspectives and cultures, in other words differences in interpretation. Always ensure that you have all the possible information from the sender before you come to a conclusion or make an interpretation. We frequently make mistakes when we communicate.

## Activity 45: General mistakes in communication

Read the following mistakes we make in communication, and indicate the ones you make regularly. Try to eliminate these mistakes and improve your communication with others.

| | |
|---|---|
| • You do not organise your thoughts before you speak. | |
| • You include too many (irrelevant) ideas in your messages. | |
| • Your statements do not contain enough information or repetition to be understandable. | |
| • You ignore the amount of information the receiver already has about the subject. | |
| • Your message is not appropriate for the frame of reference of the receiver. | |
| • You don't give your undivided attention to the sender. | |
| • You start thinking of a possible answer instead of listening to the entire message. | |
| • You listen for detail instead of the full message. | |
| • You evaluate whether the sender is right or wrong before you understand the full message correctly. | |
| • You ignore or reject the feelings and messages of others. E.g. "I don't have time." | |
| • You only give advice or false compliments. | |
| • You change or sidestep the subject easily. | |
| • You use general and unclear terms. | |
| • You are sarcastic, e.g. "Everybody knows you are never late" instead of "I feel unhappy because you are late." | |
| • You give commands, e.g. "Shut up" or "Hang up your clothes." | |
| • You threaten, e.g. "If you don't, I will . . ." | |
| • You use overgeneralisations. | |
| • You generalise, e.g. "I wish you were less cold" instead of "I wish you would smile more and talk to me (or give me a hug)." | |

| | |
|---|---|
| • You ask forgiveness for being human (imperfections). | |
| • You make assumptions rather than ensuring that you have all the facts. | |
| • You keep quiet about things which bother you or defend yourself, e.g. "You never notice what I do." | |
| • You act in rage, attack, condemn or humiliate: "This is the dumbest idea I have ever heard." | |
| • You speak on behalf of others. | |
| • You are not specific. | |
| • You interrupt others. | |
| • You complete sentences for them. | |
| • You label, e.g. "You are rude" instead of "I get irritated when you interrupt me." | |
| • You blame, e.g. "You don't care at all" instead of "I feel rejected when . . ." | |
| • You accuse, e.g. "You have never been able to handle money" instead of "I am worried because your bank account is in the red again." | |
| • You send "You should . . ." messages, e.g. "You should not feel bad" instead of "I get worried about you when you are upset." | |
| • You use emotional blocks: words which lead to negative feelings and inhibit your listening, e.g. "You never listen . . ." | |

# ACTIVITY 46: Verbal and nonverbal communication

Choose any sentence, e.g. "I don't want to work today." Say it to yourself aloud, using different tones, pitches and rhythms as well as different bodily postures. Can you see the difference in meaning in the same message?

# Activity 47: Communication self-evaluation scale

This scale [20] helps you to evaluate your current communication styles. Answer each question by drawing a circle around the number that reflects your communication style during the recent past.

| Never | | Sometimes | | Always |
|---|---|---|---|---|
| 1 | 2 | 3 | 4 | 5 |

1. I reply to questions easily. ____ 1 2 3 4 5

2. I can act self-assertively. ____ 1 2 3 4 5

3. I can demand that borrowed articles be returned without being apologetic. ____ 1 2 3 4 5

4. I can request help from others when I need it. ____ 1 2 3 4 5

5. I can tell someone when his behaviour bothers me. ____ 1 2 3 4 5

6. I can say no and refuse to do something I do not want to do. ____ 1 2 3 4 5

7. I can discuss sex with friends. ____ 1 2 3 4 5

8. I can accept being criticised. ____ 1 2 3 4 5

9. I can express my feelings directly and honestly without blaming someone else. ____ 1 2 3 4 5

10. I readily admit my mistakes. ____ 1 2 3 4 5

11. I am comfortable when addressing a group. ____ 1 2 3 4 5

12. People find it easy to chat to me. ____ 1 2 3 4 5

13. People like me. ____ 1 2 3 4 5

14. I feel that people understand me. ____ 1 2 3 4 5

15. I can express my thoughts clearly and simply. ____ 1 2 3 4 5

If most of your answers are between 1 and 2, and your total score is less than 45, you perhaps need to learn how to communicate your needs more honestly and openly.

You have to be empathetic in order to establish a good, effective relationship.

## WHAT IS EMPATHY?

You try to put yourself into the world, thoughts and feelings of another person, as he experiences them and not as you want to see them. You want to be in another person's shoes. Your attitude is one of warmth, understanding and acceptance. To be empathetic you have to think before you answer, give accurate, clear answers and react regularly in a conversation, even if it is only a nod or a "hmm". Ask if you are uncertain about the feelings of the other person. Give the correct names for feelings. The goal of empathy is to come to an understanding of the world of another person, to support the person, to avoid misunderstandings and to encourage the person to talk about his/her problems. Empathy is applicable to positive emotions as well.

There is a difference between sympathy and empathy, e.g. sympathy – "I think it is going to hurt." Empathy – "You look afraid. Are you? Let me explain what is going to happen." Empathy is the ability to know what another person feels without his saying it in words.

Practise using this sentence: **"You feel . . . (name of feeling) because . . . (reason for feeling)."** Listen to identify the underlying feelings: "It sounds as if you are disappointed."

Show understanding and attunement. However, be careful of saying "I understand." Do you really understand? Clarify and paraphrase: "Did you really feel insulted?" It should, however, not sound as if you are accusing or questioning the other person. Give your full attention to him and stop all other activities. Maintain eye contact. If it is a child you are talking to, ensure that you communicate at his level. You need to have a genuine wish to understand.

**The following are phrases you can use instead of "You feel . . .":**

It is important for you to . . .
As I understand . . .
So you feel . . .
Are you saying . . . ?
If I understand you correctly . . .
According to you . . .
It seems as if . . .
What you mean is . . .
You think . . .
I am not sure, but . . .
It makes you feel as if . . .
What bothers you . . .
It sounds to me as if you are saying . . .
From what you say it sounds as if . . .

Examples: "From what you are saying to me it sounds as if you are discouraged when you keep on trying without any visible progress."

"It makes you feel rejected if I do not talk to you."

"Help me never to judge another until I have walked two weeks in his shoes."
*Anonymous*

## How do I pay attention empathetically?

Be attuned to the other person – give him your full attention and stop all other activities.

Your body language should be one of involvement, described as follows:

**Basic elements of physical attention:**
• Sit relatively close to the other person (it should still feel comfortable);
• Maintain eye contact naturally (not for longer than 10 seconds at a time);
• Open posture (don't cross your arms and legs);
• Lean a little forward;
• Stay relaxed;
• Sit about 45 to 90 degrees in relation to the other person; not directly in front of or next to him.

## How do I listen with empathy?

There is a difference between hearing and listening. To listen with empathy means that you want to understand the meaning of the words and the feelings and you have an attitude of respect. This kind of listening is a skill that has to be learnt. There are certain filters that are applicable to listening: you hear only what you want to hear, you listen with certain prejudices, you don't listen to feelings and you are thinking about other things.[21]

Don't interrupt the other person or complete his sentences for him. Listen for feelings. What feelings underlie his words? Listen to the content of what is being said (who, what, when, where, why and how?). His tone of voice and body language (gestures and facial expressions) are important as well. What does his nonverbal communication give away about him? Does he have nervous gestures, which could mean that he is tense? Be careful not to come to conclusions that are not well founded. Encourage the person to speak with words like "So?", etc. Remember that the average person speaks about 150-200 words per minute, while your brain processes about 650 words per minute. This explains why your thoughts wander and why you have to listen consciously.

Your own posture is important as well. Does it look as if you are interested, or do you look bored? Listen to understand and not to answer. The other person frequently just wants to be heard and does not expect advice. See the world as the other person sees it – get into his shoes. Listen with an open mind (open filters), which means that you should not judge the other person or let your own assumptions stand in the way. Empathy is *not* evaluating, asking too many questions, interpreting, interrupting, judging or reasoning.

"Of course it is important to understand our fellow human being. But our understanding only bears fruit if it is supported by empathy in joy and sadness."
*Albert Einstein*

## ACTIVITY 48: Listening skills

Read the statement below and, without reading it again, answer the questions according to what you have heard.

Listen for the
- who (was involved)?
- what (happened)?
- where (did it happen)?

- how (did the person feel)?
- why (reason)?
- when (time, day)?

**Statement:**

"I want your report on the new project on my desk first thing on Monday morning. Prepare three copies because we will discuss it at the meeting on Tuesday."

**Question:**

Who: _____
_____

What: _____
_____

Where: _____
_____

How: _____
_____

Why: _____
_____

When: _____
_____

## ACTIVITY 49: Listening

Ask someone to do this activity with you. One of you must name ten of your best qualities in sixty seconds. The other person has to repeat what he has heard. (Most of the time the listener won't be able to repeat all ten, because he has started to think about his own ten best qualities which he was planning to name when it came to his turn, or he could not think of ten qualities.) It is really difficult to keep listening and not to start thinking about your own answers.

# HOW TO EXPRESS YOUR FEELINGS

Emotional literacy means that you are able to identify your feelings precisely and that you can communicate them. It also means that you have a good vocabulary of feeling words and that you are aware that feelings can differ in intensity. (See the list of feelings in the first chapter.)

It is very important that you use **"I-messages"** in your communication. Learn the following phrase: **"I feel . . . (name of feeling) because . . . (reason for feeling)"** or
**"I feel . . . because . . . and I would prefer that . . ."**
Examples of this are the following:

"I feel afraid when you are late, because I am not sure whether or not you were in an accident."
"I begin to feel overwhelmed."
"I feel rejected – can you say it differently or is that how you meant it?"

The value of "I-messages" is the following:

- Other people can understand you better and it is easier for them to empathise with you. This prevents misunderstandings and conflict.
- The other person does not feel threatened and will not withdraw, defend himself or attack you. Messages like "You irritate me when . . ." or "You should not . . ." cut communication and the person experiences you as attacking him.

The nonverbal expression of warmth, e.g. an open, warm body posture and eye contact is important when you talk about feelings.

## How to sabotage the language of feelings [22]

Avoid the following ways of expressing your feelings, as they tend to produce a negative reaction rather than a positive one where you are understood and supported.

- You mask the real feeling – disguise it or lie about it, e.g. "I hope he is not cross with me" instead of "I am afraid that he may be cross with me."
- Your verbal and nonverbal messages are not consistent. You tell someone that you love him, but your

posture is cold and aloof.
- You abuse the feeling word for the wrong reasons, e.g. "I love vegetables and I love you." Rather say: "I like vegetables." A loved one should be the only one to enjoy the words: "I love you."
- You may exaggerate (lie about) the feeling to gain attention. People find this unacceptable. This happens when you exaggerate something which happened to you, e.g. "I have completely gone to pieces" instead of "I feel shocked." You may minimise the feeling and say that it is not important, e.g. "It was not that serious."
- It is wrong to verbalise feelings by using accusations, sarcasm, and questions, such as:
  "You should have given attention to it a long time ago. You know that it made me feel neglected."
  "You don't even care if I feel sad."
  "I don't get hurt, you know."
  "Can you imagine how I feel as a result of your behaviour?"

## The indirect way to express feelings

Misunderstandings can be created when feelings are not expressed directly and this can harm relationships. A feeling is not expressed directly/clearly when words other than a feeling word are used to describe or explain the feeling. Usually secondary feelings are explained in this way. You use the following erroneously as the "I feel . . ." is not followed by a feeling word. This is the indirect way of expressing feelings and is incorrect in terms of emotional literacy.

Label: "I feel *like* an idiot."
Thought: "I feel *that* it was wrong."
Behaviour: "I feel *as if* I could strangle him."

The following are direct expressions of feelings: (the word "feel" is followed by a feeling word)

"I feel *unhappy* because I made a mistake."
"I feel *upset* because everything was wrong."
"I feel *furious* and wish I could strangle him."

In the examples above there is no doubt about the feeling which the person is experiencing. Learn and use the feeling words so that you can communicate your feelings clearly.

## ACTIVITY 50: Direct expression of feelings

Study the examples below and indicate where feelings are expressed directly/clearly (+) and where indirectly/unclearly (x):

1. "I feel like a complete idiot because I did not do it." ____

2. "I feel absolutely furious because he did not show up." ____

3. "I feel that he acted wrongly." ____

4. "I feel as if I could strangle her." ____

5. "I feel on top of the world." ____

6. "I feel very happy." ____

7. "I feel that you trust me." ____

8. "I feel as if I want to cry my eyes out." ____

9. "I feel excited." ____

10. "I feel that I want to cry." ____

The next section, which focuses on validation and invalidation of feelings, is very important, because it is so easy to make mistakes, even when we mean to do good and to comfort someone. Study this section carefully and evaluate your own communication style in relation to it.

## VALIDATION OF FEELINGS

Ensure that you understand the difference between validation and invalidation. Validation of feelings means that you accept another person's feelings and that you let him feel free to experience and express them. You show empathy, pay attention to and listen to the person. Use the phrase: "You feel . . . because . . ." You show the person that you care and that you feel attuned to him. It is safe for the person to express his feelings and the communication is strengthened.

## INVALIDATION OF FEELINGS

This means that a person's feelings are rejected, ignored, minimised, mocked or judged. The feelings of the person are disapproved of and the person feels abnormal for feeling the way he does. The negative consequence of invalidation is that communication is hampered, and someone whose feelings are not validated will not have the confidence to share them with you again. We often mean good by doing it, because we want the person to feel better – we want to get rid of the unpleasant feeling, possibly because we feel uncomfortable with it as well. Your good intentions

are negative for the person as he feels that you have no understanding of his situation and feelings. Feelings are the deepest expression of our uniqueness. Invalidation hurts us deeply.

### Ways to invalidate a feeling

The following are examples of invalidation of feelings:[23]

* You tell someone not to feel the way he does, e.g. "You should not feel so sad."
* Feelings are prescribed, e.g. "You should feel thankful"; "Don't be so sensitive."
* Feelings are ignored and/or judged.
* You make the other person feel abnormal for feeling the way he does, e.g. "One should not get upset about something like that."
* You use clichés or philosophise, e.g. "Everything will be all right" or "Tomorrow it will be better."
* When you minimise you own or another's feelings, e.g. "It was not that bad."
* When you judge or label the person, e.g. "Crybaby!" This is very negative if it is said to a boy.
* You change the subject and blame the other person, e.g. "What is wrong with you?"
* You defend the "enemy" or third party, e.g. "I think your boss is right to be cross with you."
* Sarcasm and mockery, e.g. "Oh, are you angry again?"
* You make the person feel guilty, e.g. "You should feel thankful for what I have done for you."
* When someone disregards positive feelings with a remark like: "Enjoy it – it will not last long."

## Dangers of invalidation

A person whose feelings are not validated defends himself. This may give rise to confusion, lowered self-worth and loss of self-confidence. The person does not trust himself. There are a lot of negative consequences in the long term with parent/child relationships and the relationship between husband and wife. The more sensitive the person, the more damage invalidation can do, e.g. with a child. A child would rather believe an adult than his own awareness and feelings. He may get confused between his feelings and those which the adult tells him to feel or not to feel. This is regarded as emotional abuse.

**Remember:**
First accept the person and his feelings and then address the behaviour, e.g. "You are very sorry about what happened, but you realise that you were irresponsible." Validation does not mean that you agree with the person, but it opens the communication channels in order for you to stay tuned to one another. Logical reasoning does not solve emotional problems. People want to be heard rather than to have their problems discussed in detail. Feelings are real and part of each person – we cannot deny them. People even envy others their positive feelings! Invalidation can apply to positive feelings as well.

***Do you abuse someone by denying his or her feelings and by invalidation?***

## ACTIVITY 51: Validation and invalidation

Read the statement below and indicate whether the different responses to it suggest/represent validation or invalidation of feelings.

"I am very sad as a result of his behaviour. It looks as if he is blaming me for what happened, while my intentions were good. I did not intend to do him any harm."

1. "Pull yourself together and forget about it."

2. "You are very upset about what has happened."

3. "His behaviour seems unfair to you."

4. "Don't be so sensitive."

5. "Tomorrow things will be better."

6. "You feel hurt because he blames you for everything."

7. "I think he is right to blame you for it."

8. "Perhaps you should not have done it, he gets upset so easily."

9. "It appears to me that you are really sad. Please tell me what happened."

## ACTIVITY 52: Implementation of communication skills

Indicate in the table below when and how you apply the skills and what the consequences are.

| Skills | Situation (who and what) | Your behaviour (action and words) | Consequences of your behaviour (positive/ negative) in the situation |
|---|---|---|---|
| **Paying attention:** Eye contact, positive posture which indicates your interest. Stopping all other activities. | | | |
| **Listening:** Listening to words and feelings. Listening to understand and not to answer. | | | |
| **Empathy:** Putting yourself in someone else's shoes to better understand his frame of reference and perspective. | | | |
| **"I-messages":** "I feel . . . because . . ." enhance relationships and lessen conflict. | | | |
| **Validation:** Showing empathy and giving people the freedom to experience and express their feelings. | | | |

## SUMMARY

In this chapter we discussed the most important aspects of communication. It is important to remember that misunderstandings can easily arise during communication and that you have to ask for confirmation of your interpretations of another's behaviour and feelings. You have to ensure that you understand how other people interpret your behaviour. Do they understand you correctly?

Ensure that you understand the difference between validation and invalidation and that you are able to identify the concepts in general social situations. Practise your new communication skills daily in order to integrate them.

The next very important section deals with emotional control; in other words the skills of emotionally intelligent people which enable them to cope with their emotions constructively. These people do not become victims of their own emotions.

# CHAPTER 5
## emotional control

Emotional control is one of the most important aspects of emotional intelligence. A person who is in control of his feelings is a person who is able to cope with any situation with a certain amount of confidence. He/she does not float in a sea of emotions, but is aware of the feelings which he/she experiences and knows how to cope with them. Emotional control may look easy, but it takes practice to form new patterns and behaviour. No matter how hard we try, we may lose emotional control every now and then. Acknowledge the problem, say you are sorry, and use humour to save the situation.

## GENERAL GUIDELINES FOR EMOTIONAL CONTROL

The first step in controlling your feelings is to recognise the importance of control and then to decide to control your feelings. The next step is to identify the feelings within you and to acknowledge their existence. Accept your feelings, understand why you are experiencing them and ask yourself what is the best way to cope. There should be a balance between what you think and feel. You have to feel in such a way that it does not overwhelm you. The intensity of your emotional reaction has to be in line with the preceding situation. This means that it may or should differ from situation to situation, depending on your interpretation of the event. Use your feelings constructively; in other words, decide what will be the best reaction to a certain feeling which will lead to positive consequences. Try to make the best of the situation. First you have to try to relieve/control the feeling by changing your thoughts (viewpoint) about the situation. If you are unsuccessful, you should use one of the techniques (which will be discussed in this chapter) to change/control the intensity of the feeling.

**How did your family cope with emotions?** In other words, what did your grandparents/parents/brothers/sisters do with their feelings? The answer to this question may give you valuable insights into the way you cope with your own emotions, since you often learn positive and negative behavioural patterns by example.

It is important to remember that you alone are responsible for your feelings. Nobody can "make" you experience certain feelings. You can't say to someone: "You are making me angry" or "You make me unhappy." You should have control over your feelings. This is applicable to your reactions to the feelings as well. Always try to think about your feelings and the events that gave rise to them before you react. Therefore, there should be a time lapse between your experience of the feelings and your reaction. This time lapse gives you the opportunity to think logically about the events and to make a choice. There should always be a conscious thought process between the feeling and the behaviour.

It looks like this: **event** (someone criticises you) → immediate **interpretation/thought** (He does not like me or I am not good enough) → **feelings** (humiliated, inferior) → **choice** (logical thinking, such as "It is not valid criticism.") → **reaction** (ignore the criticism or assert yourself).

It is important for even positive feelings to be controlled – enthusiasm may lead to impulsive behaviour that may have negative consequences. It does not mean that positive feelings should not be intensely enjoyed – just think for a moment before you react impulsively.

Feelings and the reaction to them are not the same. If you are furious, it does not mean that you have to slam the door. It is important that feelings are always expressed in an appropriate way, at the right time and with the right words. You will only succeed if you give yourself time to think and choose the correct reaction/response.

Emotional control is one trait of emotional intelligence which has to be put carefully into perspective. It certainly does not mean that you should suppress or deny your feelings. What it does mean is that you should become aware of or recognise the emotion and know how to cope with it in the best way possible. You have to show a certain amount of emotional reaction in terms of the specific situation. Think of emotions as emotional coins in your body. For every situation where you experience emotions you have to spend a few coins. Do you want to pay more for a certain piece of clothing or object than it is worth? No, you want to pay a reasonable amount. How do we determine a reasonable emotional price? Dr Tom Miller,[24] an American, thought about a very meaningful way to determine a reasonable emotional reaction to a particular situation. Remember that if you overreact it will not help to change the situation; so why pay such a high emotional price?

We will explain this now. According to Miller, you have to start by giving yourself a scale or something you can compare your emotional pain to. Remember that this is an abstract concept which will probably be different for everybody. An important goal of the process is that when you create the scale you start to think cognitively. This might lessen the intensity of the emotional experience. You start to think logically and thus establish a balance between your emotions and your thoughts.

Make a list of emotional events that test your being in control. The list below provides only examples – you can extend the list of physical injuries according to your frame of reference. When you find yourself in an intense emotional situation, ask yourself a question like this: Is it really so unacceptable to me when someone jumps the queue that I am willing to pay a physical price for it? Which physical price are you willing to pay in order to remove the emotional situation? Would you be willing to dislocate an ankle to prevent someone from jumping the queue? If your answer is "no", go down on your scale. Are you willing to get a scratch to prevent the situation? Keep on with this process until you reach a point on the scale which you can accept in order to get rid of the emotional event. When you have reached that point, e.g. you are willing to get a scratch (4%), say to yourself: "This event had to happen (because it did) and it is 4% bad. I can cope with 4%." The worst physical injury you can endure is 100%. You have to decide how terrible a specific situation is in terms of a percentage of physical injury. Remember, the moment that you overreact you might find yourself withdrawing or behaving in such a way that you are humiliated. You might say something to the person who jumps the queue which will draw the attention of other people.

Example:

| List of emotional events: | Physical injuries: |
| --- | --- |
| Most terrible emotional event | 100% Maximum physical pain |
| Death of a loved one | 99% Serious burn wounds |
| Any negative emotion at home | 85% Lose an arm or leg |
| Lose your job | 50% Fracture |
| Divorce | 20% Dislocate you ankle |
| Any negative emotion at work | 15% You have the measles |
| The key is locked in your car | 10% Cut on your leg |
| Have to stand in a queue | 5% Four stitches |
| Someone jumps the queue | 4% Scratch |
| Continuous negative situation, e.g. someone who drives very badly | 3% Bruise |

## WAYS IN WHICH EMOTIONS CAN BE CONTROLLED

There are different ways in which you can control your emotions.

### Becoming emotionally aware

Be aware of your own emotions. The higher your emotional awareness, the better you are prepared to recognise emotions and to react correctly to them. Try to distinguish between primary and secondary emotions in order to react appropriately.

### Physical exercise

Exercise helps with controlling and relieving emotions, as each feeling is associated with certain physiological changes in the body. Thinking rationally about your feelings will not relieve your physical symptoms, but exercising will help to restore the physiological balance. Any reasonably intense physical exercise will control your feelings. It has the added benefit of releasing more "feeling good" enzymes in your body. If you can do some exercises to music, you get energy from the music as well. Always start slowly with a new exercise programme and visit your doctor if you are uncertain about your medical condition. Here are some exercises you can do:

• It is important to stretch your calf muscles, as they become shorter and stiff when you are under stress. (This prepares your body for the fight of flight reaction.)

• Do some side-to-side and up-and-down movements with your head (not backwards) and relax your shoulders as much as possible. Be careful with this if you have problems with your neck. Our neck and shoulder muscles tend to get stiff very quickly when we experience intense feelings.

• This is not really an exercise, but always try to lift your eyes when you experience feelings of sadness and depression. The moment you look up, you have more access to your higher brain and you can think more logically.

• Stamp your feet on the ground or punch a pillow when you are angry. Walk quickly on the same spot or go for a walk.

It is claimed that acupuncture can relieve certain feelings. Contact people who do this professionally for more information.

### Think logically

Try to distance yourself from your feelings and identify the problem that gave rise to them. Don't ignore the feelings – be aware of them while you try to write down solutions. Is it possible that your assumptions, prejudices and preconceived ideas could have contributed to your feelings? If so, reformulate them in order to experience more positive feelings.

In order to control your emotions and regain access to your cognitive processes, you can do one or more of the following:

1. Compile a list of the names of six magazines;
2. Verbalise the telephone numbers of two of your best friends; or
3. Add the numbers of the number plates of the cars in front of you, or
4. Think of the names of six people whom you have spoken to recently.

### Robot technique

Use the **Robot technique**[25] of Stop → Think → Do in order to control your feelings.

## ROBOT TECHNIQUE FOR EMOTIONAL CONTROL

1. STOP > CALM DOWN. THINK BEFORE YOU ACT.

2. THINK > NAME THE PROBLEM. HOW DO YOU FEEL?
3. FORMULATE POSITIVE GOALS.
4. THINK ABOUT SOLUTIONS.
5. WHAT WILL THE CONSEQUENCES BE?

6. DO > GO ON AND TRY THE BEST PLAN.

Exercise this technique by visualising the lights on a robot. When you find yourself in a situation where you need emotional control, you will be able to see the lights in your imagination. This is a sign to you that it is a potentially dangerous situation, especially if you tend to act impulsively. It can also indicate to you that there are other possibilities to consider and only then are you free to react.

### Rubber band

Put a rubber band around your wrist and shoot yourself with it as soon as you feel you are losing control. This will encourage you to think logically about the situation. A tap on your leg will have the same result.

### Visualisation

Visualisation is a technique you can use which has positive results. You can visualise yourself coping with a feeling and through this prepare yourself to cope with it in a real situation. Remember that your brain cannot distinguish between imagination and reality. If you feed your brain positive, successful images, it will function in such a way as to make the images come true. You are visualising if you are in calm, positive surroundings and you imagine how it will feel, look,

sound, taste and smell when you have coped with the feeling and have reacted to it in the correct way. You have to visualise how others will give you feedback: what do they say and how do they behave towards you? How do you give yourself positive feedback? Do the visualisation for at least ten minutes with closed eyes. Practise it in rich detail. The more focused and persistent the visualisation, the quicker and more effective it will be. When you are in a situation where you have to control your emotions, visualise a previous situation in which you have coped successfully. Remember that visualisation is an art and some people find it easier than others. Put some effort into mastering this skill. World-class athletes visualise themselves performing: they see it, feel it and experience it before they begin. This has proved to be very important in their exercise programme.

## ACTIVITY 53: Visualisation

Use the following visualisation to gain control of your emotions and to relax. Take a deep breath and close your eyes. Imagine that you are on the beach of a tropical island. You are alone. You can hear the thundering of the waves and the seagulls in the distance. The rays of the sun feel warm on your body and you can feel the texture of the sand against your body and under your feet. You like the sensation. You smell the salty air. There is nothing you are worried about and you can feel how relaxed your body feels. The moment is there for you to enjoy and you may enjoy it when you want to and for as long as you want to.

### Progressive muscle relaxation

You gain a heightened state of relaxation when you contract your muscles beyond their normal tension and release them. Frequently you only realise how tense you really are when you do this exercise. It may be difficult for you at first to isolate the specific muscles, but you will soon be able to do it. Contracting your muscles should be done in a certain fixed sequence. Lie comfortably on your back. Start with your toes, then your feet, your ankles, calves, knees, thighs, buttocks, stomach, chest, back, shoulders, arms and hands. Then contract your neck and facial muscles and lastly the muscles around your eyes.

Then relax all the muscles. All the muscles must be contracted for a few seconds before you release them, and only then start with the next muscle group. When you have done all the muscle groups, try to contract all of the muscles once or twice at the same time and then relax. Turn on your side and enjoy the relaxed state your body is in. If you are in a situation where it is impossible to do the full exercise (such as in a traffic jam), contract all of the muscles at the same time and fully release them. This shortened exercise may have the same results as the other one, but it is better to do the longer one when you are able to.

## Empty chair technique

A technique which you may find useful is to sit in a quiet room next to an empty chair. Imagine that the problem or person involved with the emotion is sitting in the chair. Talk in detail about it and say how you see the situation. Verbalise your specific primary and secondary feelings with the correct intensity as well.

## Keep a journal of your feelings

When you experience intense emotions, write them down in detail. Ensure that you write down their intensity (1-10) as well. All negative feelings and thoughts must be written down. This gives you a better perspective on your experiences.

## Paint/draw your feelings

Painting or drawing your feelings gives you the opportunity to release excessive energy creatively and enables you to acknowledge and accept the feeling.

## Try to see the humour in the feeling and the situation

Someone who can look at his life, problems and feelings with humour is more capable of having control over negative events. Humour brings another perspective and heightened energy. Be creative in your humour.

## Think of an animal or event in nature that describes your feeling best

With which animal would you associate your feeling? Is it a lion or a snake? Describe the comparison between the feeling and the characteristics of the animal in detail.

Or do you feel like a volcano which is about to erupt? Your feelings may be like a flood that swamps everything around it.

## Make animal sounds!

Go to a place where you can make a noise and imitate the animal you have identified in the previous activity. Try to do it as realistically as possible.

## Deep breathing

Breathing deeply relieves tension and gives you a few moments to think clearly. When you experience intense feelings, breathe deeply. It is nearly impossible to experience the feelings while you are breathing deeply. Practise like this:

- Sit erect in a comfortable chair or stand erect and relax.
- Become aware of your breathing. Breathe deeply and slowly.
- Close your eyes and breathe in through your nose. Let the air fill the lower parts of your lungs. Your stomach and diaphragm will move outwards to make room for the air. Then fill the middle parts of your lungs while your ribs and chest move out. Then fill the upper parts as well. Do this as a continuous action as you breathe in.
- Hold your breath for a few seconds.
- Blow slowly out through your nose and feel how the tension is released.
- Keep doing this for five minutes.
- Open your eyes and stay in the same position for a while.
- If you start feeling light-headed, breathe normally again.
- Resume your daily tasks.

## *Brain gym*

This involves exercises to keep your brain awake. It is important for your brain to function at its best for you to reach your full potential. Movement enhances your blood circulation and lets you breathe more deeply, with the result that more oxygen is taken to the cells. The messages between the brain and the body will move more easily. Since water is an electrical impulse conductor, it is essential to drink enough water. Below are examples of exercises which you should do daily for at least two months in order to enhance your ability to control your emotions.[26]

### Brain buttons

Place one hand on your navel (this stimulates balance) and, using the thumb and index finger of your other hand, stimulate the two hollows just under your collarbone, on either side of your breastbone.

### Double doodle

Keeping your head still, focus on both hands as you simultaneously "draw" large circles that are mirror images of each other. When your hands work easily together, but in opposite directions, you will make large, free-form, symmetrical doodle patterns.

### Grounder

Stand with your feet comfortably apart, one foot pointing forwards and the other to the side. Bend the knee of the foot pointing to the side and move sideways until your knee is in line with your toes. Keep your body upright throughout. Hold this position for 8 seconds and return to the starting position. Do a few movements to both sides, remembering to keep your shoulders in line with your hips.

### Energiser

Sit comfortably on a chair, head bent and back hunched, and place your hands (fingertips facing) on the table. Breathe in deeply and slowly as you raise your head and eyes, straightening your back. Breathe out slowly as you lower your head. Relax. Repeat several times.

## Hook-up

Sit or lie comfortably with your ankles crossed. Stretch your arms out in front of you, the backs of your hands together and your thumbs facing downwards. Turn your hands so that your palms are together and interlace your fingers. Bend your hands down and inwards towards your chest until you are sitting like the figure in the illustration. Relax your shoulders and place your tongue against the highest part of your palate. Breathe slowly and deeply.

After several breaths, uncross your hands and ankles, rest your fingertips against one another and take a last deep breath.

## Thinking caps

Sit or stand up straight and hold your ears between your thumbs and index fingers. Massage the entire ear firmly a few times, from top to bottom. Your ears could become red and warm as a result of the increased bloodflow and neural stimulation.

### *Coping with your feelings in view of your brain profile*

As discussed in Chapter 2 (see p. 69) there are certain specific tasks/activities which you can do to bring relief from intense emotions. These are *inter alia*: touching, exercise, visualisation and music for the receptive person, and role-playing, screaming, crying, sighing, laughing, singing, drawing and moving for the expressive person.

### *Diet and emotional control*

What you eat has a direct influence on your feelings (mood), energy levels, thinking processes, sleeping habits, stress levels, etc. The food you eat forms the building blocks of the neurotransmitters involved in brain activity. It is especially the peptides, steroids, serotonin, dopamine, norepinephrine and acetylcholine that are important. The following foods are important: whole-wheat bread and other whole-wheat products, bran, soup, fruit like bananas, pears, strawberries and mangoes, nuts, vegetables like carrots, broccoli, beans, potatoes and spinach, low fat milk, cheese and yoghurt, peanut butter, popcorn, garlic, ham, fish and chicken. You can also take a multivitamin and mineral supplement that contains calcium, magnesium, vitamin B (1, 2, 6 and 12) and zinc.

It will help you if you can keep a journal of your feelings before and after you have eaten certain foods to evaluate the impact that they have on you. Your diet plays a very important role in your emotional control if you suffer from premenstrual tension (PMT). Magnesium is one of the supplements prescribed for the prevention and treatment of PMT, while women experiencing PMT should eliminate sugar.[27]

More adventurous people can use extracts of flowers. It is alleged that these extracts do not cause any side effects and that they may improve your mood within several weeks. Examples are the following: aspen for fears, *Impatiens* for impatience and irritability and the "Rescue Remedy" which is a combination of flower essences and which is used in crisis situations like shock, panic, grief and fear. Please consult your chemist for more information.

### Take time out (remove yourself from the situation)

Take time out when you realise that you are going to lose control over your emotions in a difficult situation, especially if you could lose your self-respect (and your work!) as a result. Ask to be excused and leave the room. You can stand outside and breathe deeply (see above), exercise, drink some water or go for a walk. Calm yourself and organise your thinking. Go back when you feel in control of your emotions.

## SUMMARY

The techniques described above are ways in which you can control intense emotions so that they don't disrupt your general functioning and help you regain balance between your logic and feelings. Remember that you cannot make well-considered decisions when you are experiencing intense emotions, and that the continual presence of these feelings in your body may lower your immunity and damage your health. It is therefore important that you become aware of your feelings as soon as possible, acknowledge and accept them and try to control them. Emotional control is important for maintaining your relationships. People who frequently lose control and express their emotions inappropriately may have problems in establishing good relations with others.

We want to stress again that control of emotions does not mean suppressing them. It means that you become aware of your feelings to such an extent that you can choose the most appropriate way to react. You may find yourself in situations where you cannot cry about something you have heard or experienced. Emotional control is necessary until you reach a safe place where you can express your feelings.

The following chapter focuses on coping with certain exhausting feelings.

# CHAPTER 6
## coping with some tiring feelings

In this chapter we will focus on some common feelings which may be difficult to cope with, e.g. anger, worry/fear and stress. As it is not possible to discuss every unpleasant feeling, we will only focus on these. It is important that you are continually aware of your feelings and that you are in control of them. We will first discuss anger.

## ANGER

Do the following activity (54) and then carefully read the theory about anger.

### Coping with your own anger

Identify the correct person who caused your anger. It is important to remember that anger is a secondary feeling and it is your responsibility to identify the primary feeling. Recognise and acknowledge the feeling:

"I am angry." You will not be able to cope with the feeling unless you have acknowledged it. Determine the intensity of the feeling. Are you really furious or are you just angry? Try to establish the cause of the feeling, in other words, the primary feeling and the unmet needs. What gave rise to your experiencing the primary feeling? Share the feeling with the person involved with the help of an "I-message", e.g. "I feel very hurt and angry because you insulted me in front of my friends. If you ever have to do it again I would prefer it if you did it when we are alone." Express the feeling physically by exercising or going for a walk. You might like to punch a pillow. While you are experiencing the anger, you might ask the other person to excuse you and resume the discussion later. While you are alone, you can do some of the relaxation exercises or the other techniques discussed in the previous chapter.

---

## ACTIVITY 54: "My anger"

1. It angers me when

_____

_____

2. I get extremely angry when

_____

_____

3. When I experience rage,

_____

_____

4. After expressing my anger, I

_____

_____

5. After having being exposed to someone's rage, I feel

_____

_____

6. I express my anger and rage by

_____

_____

7. After expressing my anger, others feel

_____

_____

## *How do I cope with another person's anger?*

When you are exposed to someone else's anger:

- Never get involved in another person's anger unnecessarily. Don't take sides.
- Acknowledge the feeling of the other person – validate it. "You are extremely angry. Should I phone next time to let you know I will be late?"
- Accept responsibility for your part in the other person's feelings.
- Remember that feelings are contagious. It is very important to say to yourself as soon as possible: "He is furious, but that does not mean that I will become furious as well. I want to stay calm. I am going to breathe deeply and speak slowly."

- If you cannot stay calm, become aware of what is happening inside yourself and acknowledge your own feeling: "I am getting angry."
- Stick to the same phrase: "If you calm down, I will listen to you." Repeat it until the other person has calmed down. If it does not happen, excuse yourself (take time out).
- Ask for clarification about the needs and expectations of the other person. Verify the facts. Open your filters and try to stay objective.
- Stick to your values – don't let feelings of guilt or loyalty get you into trouble. Repair the relationship and admit it if you are sorry, then apologise.

## ACTIVITY 55: Behaviour and feelings as a result of anger in a relationship

Which of the following reactions occur frequently in your relationships? Mark them. Work towards preventing anger in your relationships, talk about and eliminate the anger.

| | | | |
|---|---|---|---|
| The need always to be correct | | Negative language | |
| Negative criticism | | Moaning | |
| Judgement/condemnation | | Pessimistic attitude | |
| Threats | | Comparisons | |
| Emotional explosions | | Blaming | |
| Questioning | | Attacks | |
| Labelling | | Mind reading | |
| Insensitivity/no interest | | Giving commands/orders | |
| Lies | | Pretending | |
| Jealousy | | Punishing | |

If you do not address the anger in your relationships, some of the following may occur. Indicate those present in your relationships.

| Suspicion | | Loneliness | |
|---|---|---|---|
| Frustration | | Inferiority | |
| Hopelessness | | Rejection | |
| Fear | | Inadequacy | |
| Guilt | | Envy | |
| Hostility | | Impatience | |
| Jealousy | | Boredom | |

Anger coped with constructively gives rise to positive feelings like optimism and you may experience increased energy and self-worth. Therefore it is important to discuss and let go of the anger that is present between you and other people.

"If you are angry with someone else, you allow them to live rent-free in you mind."
*Antoine De Saint-Exupéry*

## WORRY/FEAR

To worry about something is a very paralysing experience that uses a lot of energy. It may prevent you from gaining clarity about your problems. Fear is linked to worry: fear is frequently a more intense form of worry.

### Why am I constantly worried about something?

People frequently worry constantly or feel anxious about something. Sometimes they cannot say what is worrying them – it may be a vague feeling of restlessness or it may be an anxious feeling which hampers their general functioning and drains their energy. The following are some tips for coping with this feeling of worry:

### Tips to overcome worry

Do the following if you tend to worry:
1. Write down precisely what you worry about. (Be very precise – the problem often looks less intimidating once it is written down in detail.) "Laddering" is the technique you can use to get to the core of the problem. Use this to get to the bottom of your deepest worry, in order for you to cope with it (make a plan and do something about it), and to question your irrational fears.
   The following is an example of laddering:

"I am worried that I may lose my job."

**What will happen then?**

↓ "I will lose my income."

**What will happen then?**

↓ "My wife will divorce me."

**What will happen then?**

↓ "I will be alone."

**What will happen then?**

↓ "I will be very lonely."

**What will happen then?**

→ "I will be worthless and will give up on everything."

Ask yourself: what are the chances that you will lose your job? If you do, what are the alternatives? Will you be able to get another job or could you start your own business? Will your wife really divorce you? How have you coped with loneliness in the past? Do you give up this easily? Are you capable of starting again?

Make a habit of questioning your fears. It might be a reality that you could lose your job and that you might experience a lot of uncertainty about it. The art is in staying rational and being prepared with a plan of action should something happen. Evaluate why you are afraid of losing your job. What are the reasons? Maybe you know that a certain percentage of the employees will be retrenched and that you may be one of them. You may feel inadequate as well, or your employer is possibly not satisfied with your performance. Evaluate your alternatives when you get to the real reason – can you be transferred to another division? Can you do a course to improve your performance? Is it possible for you and your employer to discuss the problem in depth? By thinking about your fear in this rational way, you may come to a positive solution that would not be possible if your irrational thoughts and fears ran rampant.

2. Write down what you can do about the real problem.

3. Decide what you want to do about it and which skills you have to cope with it.

4. Start immediately to implement your decision.[28]

5. Relax. Do the activities discussed in the previous chapter.

6. Put your problems into perspective. Will I still worry about this problem in two months' time?

7. Write down what you are worrying about on a piece of paper. Put the paper in a drawer and only look at it again after a few weeks. If you are still worried put it back in the drawer. If not, tear it up. (Time solves a lot of problems.)

8. Accept the worst that could happen. Accept the inevitable and learn to live with it.

9. Live from day to day. Don't try to solve tomorrow's problems today.

10. Exercise. Take deep breaths.

11. What are the chances, according to the law of averages, that this that I am worried about, will actually happen? It is a fact that 90% of the things we worry about will not come true.

12. Determine the amount of dismay/worry the situation is worth. Decide not to be more upset than this. (Compare it with the general guidelines on emotional control in the previous chapter, p. 98.)

13. Draw up a prioritised list of things you are worried about. Visualise each situation and give it an alternative consequence (positive result).

## ACTIVITY 56: How to cope with constant worry

Do this activity with regard to **each situation** that you are concerned about, in order to gain clarity and be motivated to do something about it.

1. Write down precisely what you are worried about. Use the laddering technique.

_____

_____

_____

2. What are the chances, according to the law of averages, that it will happen?

_____

_____

_____

3. What is the worst that can happen if what you are worried about comes true?

_____

_____

4. What can/will you do if it really happens?

_____

_____

5. What can you do in the meantime until what you are worrying about becomes true or not?

_____

_____

6. Is there anything that you can do about the problem to minimise its worst consequences? Can you solve the problem in the meantime?

_____

_____

### Coping with fear

You may have experienced fear frequently: You want to take a risk, but the fear of making a mistake is much bigger that the challenge of the risk. What happens then? You stay where you are and you don't take any chances. It is, however, true that you have to take risks, to try things and make mistakes in order to grow. Fear may be applicable to anything you want or have to do. The foundation of fear is your doubt about your own capabilities. Will I be able to do it? It is important that you try new things to overcome the fear of them. To do nothing as a result of fear is much more negative than trying something and perhaps making a mistake or not being successful. Be in control of your self-talk (thoughts) and assumptions/beliefs. The more constructively you can think about your own abilities, the quicker you will have the courage to start new things. Say "yes" to that which comes your way and believe that you will be able to cope with it. Don't let your fear prevent you from striving for and reaching your dreams!

"Ships in harbours are safe. But that is not what ships are made for."
*John Shedd*

## COPING WITH STRESS

Sometime during our lifetime we are all faced with a situation where we feel inadequate to cope with the demands and expectations placed on us. It is important that we stay objective and not give stress the opportunity to reduce the functions of our higher brain. You have to be able to function meaningfully and to think logically without letting stress get the better of you.

Remember that stress often results from the difference between the reality as you see it (your truth) and the reality of the world outside you. Confirm your perceptions and thoughts and ensure that you have all the necessary information before you come to any conclusions.

Keep in mind that the continual experience of stress may damage your body, as the chemical processes associated with stress may for example lower your immunity. People who experience long-term stress are much more vulnerable to illness as their bodies are not as capable of fighting it as they should be.

## *Tips for coping with stress*

1. Study the physical symptoms of stress in your body and see how quickly you are able to recognise them. The quicker you can recognise them, the greater your chances of coping effectively will be. (See Chapter 1 "What do you feel?" on p. 21.)

2. Practise deep breathing (see "Deep breathing" in the previous chapter, p. 102).

3. Visualise a situation where you were able to cope effectively with stress (see "Visualisation" on p. 101).

4. Lifestyle management. See Activities 42, 43 and 44 with regard to your activity analysis, balance and time for yourself.

5. Pay attention to your thought patterns and rephrase your distorted patterns constructively. (See "Automatic and distorted thinking patterns" in Chapter 2 on p. 57.)

6. Try to get enough sleep. People's need to sleep differs, but everyone should get between 6-8 hours sleep every night. Too little sleep may give rise to feelings of irritation, depression and decreased concentration. Sleep can restore your physical and emotional balance and gives you the energy to manage what life confronts you with.

How much stress are you trying to cope with at one time?

Do **Activity 57**: **Recognising the stress in your life** on p. 112. Doing this and knowing what stress is doing to yourself and those around you is a big step towards coping with it.

## SUMMARY

In coping with tiring emotions, it is important that you are aware of your feelings and their intensity. Secondly, you have to think logically, in order to react to the feeling in the most appropriate way. It is also essential that you know where the feeling comes from in order to pay attention to your unmet needs.

In the next chapter we concentrate on coping strategies with regard to specific situations where intense emotions often occur. Choosing happiness as an alternative is discussed.

# ACTIVITY 57: Recognising the stress in your life

Complete the following form:

| Situations/events/ problems Write down everything that is causing you stress/worries. | Physical symptoms Write down all the physical symptoms that you can recognise in your body. | External consequences Name the effect that stress has on your family, work, sport, etc. | What is the first step that you can take to alleviate stress with regard to each problem? | Determine a return date when you will have reached the previous step. |
|---|---|---|---|---|
| | | | | |
| | | | | |
| | | | | |
| | | | | |

# CHAPTER 7
## coping with specific situations

You may often find yourself in a situation which you don't know how to cope with, and which may cause strong feelings like disappointment and failure. In this chapter we discuss coping strategies (in terms of emotional intelligence) regarding criticism, conflict, setbacks, self-forgiveness and the forgiveness of others, changes and choices about life situations. At the end of the chapter we focus on happiness as a choice to triumph over your negative experiences. Let us first look at criticism.

## COPING WITH CRITICISM

Criticism may give rise to intense emotions and therefore it is important that you have the skills to deal with it.

- The first principle is not to defend yourself, deny the facts or attack the other person.
- Another important principle is to determine whether the criticism is **valid** or not. If it is valid, acknowledge it and try to change your behaviour. If it is not valid, ignore it.
- Be open to self-improvement if necessary. See it as an opportunity to grow. Draw up a plan of action to improve/change your behaviour where applicable.
- Stay calm and use the robot technique (see Chapter 5, p. 101). Play for time to calm yourself down and gain clarity. Protect yourself if you think that the time is not right – take "Time Out" if you want to. Share your reaction with the other person.
- Be rational and objective as far as possible.
- Listen carefully for the correct facts. Ask for clarification in order to prevent misunderstandings.
- Show that you have empathy with the other person: "It must frustrate you when I . . ."
- Admit it if you were wrong and apologise.
- Agree where possible – it often takes the wind out of his sails! For example, if someone tells you not to smoke, agree with him: "Yes, you are right. I should not smoke."
- Remember that you should be in control of your

feelings. No one can humiliate you without your permission! Give your self-confidence a boost. Think about all your positive traits to decrease the impact of the criticism.
- Ask the other person to say precisely what he wants from you. Ask: "How would you have done it?"
- If the criticism is not valid, give examples to indicate the opposite.
- Step into the person's personal space. It may discourage him!
- Try to determine the motives of the person who criticised you. Are there other disguised feelings and unresolved issues in your relationship which made him behave as he did?

### You as the critic

If you tend to criticise others unnecessarily and destructively, there may be several reasons for this, such as:

- It makes you feel more dignified or better than other people. You validate your own way of doing things and ignore the good in someone else's work.
- It is possible that you are protecting yourself and therefore you attack first. It helps you to ignore your own mistakes. By making others feel bad or stupid, you feel that you are in control. You are often a self-critic.
- By criticising others you keep your distance and don't let others get involved with you. You focus attention on yourself and you feel strong, as others are afraid of you.

Do you have a healthy self-worth or do you feel inferior?

Sometimes it is necessary to give constructive feedback, as in a **working situation.** The following are tips to keep in mind:

1. Identify the specific problem that you want to address.
2. Identify why it is a problem.

3. Ensure that you know how you want to convey the feedback/criticism.
4. Ensure that the time and place are suited for this.
5. Protect the other person's self-worth.
6. Emphasise the progress the person has made already.
7. Show that you care for the other person.
8. Be in control of your own feelings.
9. Suggest possible alternatives that the other person might want to choose.
10. Mention that it is your own opinion and that it may be subjective.
11. Give specific examples that indicate the problem.
12. Give positive recognition.
13. Admit that the situation is difficult.
14. Be aware of the body language of the other person. Validate his feelings.
15. Discuss possible solutions.
16. State the benefits that may be reached.
17. End on a positive note.
18. Follow up and see whether change brings about the desired results.[29]

### Why do I criticise myself and what can I do about it?

We are frequently our own worst critics! Listen to what you say to yourself and determine whether it is positive or negative. Negative assumptions/convictions about yourself are a form of self-criticism as well. Accept yourself as a unique being who may make mistakes. Remember that perfectionism is a negative, destructive personality trait.

## COPING WITH CONFLICT (PROBLEM-SOLVING)

Coping with conflict works best when:

- The parties involved are in direct communication with each other, in other words it is better to be with one another rather than trying to solve the problem by telephone;
- They can listen with empathy and validate feelings;
- They can express their thoughts and feelings;
- Needs and feelings are respected;
- Both parties have "equal" power, thus one person is not afraid of or overdependent on the other;
- There is a willingness to participate and
- The end goal is a win-win situation.

### How do you cope with conflict?

An important principle is that first you must want to understand the other person and only then try to guide him to understand you. Most conflicts are already solved as soon as both parties are able to understand each other's viewpoints. Frequently there are such high barriers between people that they cannot accept the other person as he is, and they try to change him instead of putting themselves in his shoes. Conflict decreases your energy levels for positive feelings, which means that you have to cope with conflict as soon as possible in order to be able to experience positive feelings again.

**Steps in coping with conflict**:

1. **Ensure that you understand the other person – start with the feelings**:
   Let the other person express his feelings. Validate them. Show empathy. "You feel . . . because . . ."
   Together with the other person, identify his primary feelings and unmet emotional needs (e.g. recognition, consolation). Be in control of your own feelings and make sure that you are not infected by the negative feelings. Ask the other person: "What will make you feel better?" As soon as you are sure that you understand his feelings, you can focus on your own feelings.

2. **Ensure that you are understood**:
   Share your feelings (correct names and intensity): "I feel . . . because . . ." and your unmet needs with other the person. Confirm it if he understands accurately. Say what will make you feel better. Do not attack the person with "you . . ." messages.

3. **Seek the origin of the feelings and the problem**.
   What is the problem/disputed point? Describe the problem in detail to prevent misunderstandings. Each of you should have the opportunity to describe his/her goal.

4. **Write down each person's part in the problem**.
   Determine what each does to cause or to maintain the problem.

5. **Write down what was done in the past to solve the problem but was unsuccessful.**

**6. Obtain collective options and solutions**.
Brainstorm possible solutions. A brainstorm means that as many ideas as possible should be generated in order to get to a creative solution. How is it done?

1. Think of as many ideas as possible (quantity);
2. Combine ideas and improve them;
3. Keep a visual record of the ideas (write them down);
4. Be original/creative;
5. Don't evaluate/criticise before all the ideas have been discussed.

This is the ideal time to open your filters and get some new perspectives! Discuss each alternative and your feelings about it.

**7. Choose a suitable plan of action**.
After the alternatives have been discussed, select the solution which will produce the most positive *feelings* and decide how you want to go about reaching the solution. What will each of you have to do? Plan another meeting for further discussion or evaluation of the situation.

Give yourself points for the consequences of a decision to guide you in your choices:

- If the plan of action is positive for you, give yourself 2 points.
- If it is positive for others, give yourself 1 point.
- If the plan of action has a long-term benefit for you, give yourself 2 points.
- If it has a short-term benefit, give yourself 1 point.

Try to choose the solution that means the most points for you and the other person.

**Remember:**
You have to understand the other person's thoughts, feelings and needs; his frame of reference. Do you really know how the other person sees and interprets the situation?

Role-plays work well – exchange roles. First try it with a less serious problem. The better you understand the other side of the matter (empathy), the more you will be able to solve conflict.

You don't always need to be correct or to win. Accept the other person and don't try to change him. The end goal of coping with conflict is a stronger, better relationship.

## Listen actively during a conflict situation

To stay really calm during a conflict situation is very difficult. The following are possible ideas to keep in mind:

1. Focus on the conversation and don't think about anything else.

2. Don't make any assumptions about what the other person is thinking, feeling or wanting.

3. Don't think about what you want to say before the other person has finished talking.

4. Let the other person say what he wants to say. Don't interrupt.

5. Listen for feelings and thoughts.

6. Be aware of the other person's verbal and nonverbal behaviour.

7. Show with your nonverbal behaviour that you care.

8. Use alternative listening responses like clarification, repetition, rephrasing, reflecting, etc. to bring the wishes and needs of the other person to the fore.

9. Ask questions with the aim of getting information and not criticising.

10. Be patient. Ensure that you fully understand the problem before you give any solutions.

"Confrontation doesn't always bring a solution to the problem, but until you confront the problem, there will be no solution."
*James Baldwin*

## What is your conflict style?

Most people who get involved in conflict fit into one of the following categories. Where do you fit in? Identify your style of conflict and try to change your attitude and technique as described above (in "How do you cope with conflict?" and "Listen actively during a conflict situation").

1. **The conflict avoider:** Most people who avoid conflict have problems with creating boundaries with their colleagues/family because they are not able to say "no".

2. **The passive aggressor:** They have various ways in which to show others that they are upset or that they don't agree.

3. **The overly suspicious person:** They are usually loners because they don't trust anyone.

4. **The sudden exploder:** They tend to get furious suddenly when things are not going the way they want. They are intimidating, which increases the conflict rather than solving it.

5. **The conflict creator:** They feel at home with conflict and will create it so as to be able to experience the excitement.

6. **The bully:** They expect and demand that others will do what they want. They will have temper tantrums to get others to co-operate and will attack and insult verbally.

7. **"I am so sensitive":** Fragile, oversensitive with regard to criticism, easily hurt, defensive, uncertain, shy, little self-confidence.

8. **The complainer:** Their daily pattern consists of moaning endlessly about everything.

9. **The moral crusader:** This person acts as if he knows more than anyone else does and as if he is the only one with moral principles.

10. **The grudge holder:** The grudges of this person are a major obstacle when conflict has to be resolved.[30]

## ACTIVITY 58: Conflict and criticism

Compare the way you have coped with conflict and criticism in the past with your present knowledge about it.

Choose an example of a conflict situation in which you were involved prior to studying this workbook. Describe your reactions and those of the other people involved and their consequences.

_____
_____
_____
_____
_____
_____

Think about your latest conflict situation or the one mentioned above. Write down a list of ten sentences that you could have used to achieve different (more constructive) results.

_____
_____
_____
_____
_____

Apply the robot technique in conjunction with your new knowledge to the situation and describe how you could have coped differently.

_____
_____
_____
_____
_____
_____
_____
_____
_____
_____
_____

Repeat the process for a situation in which you were criticised.

**Remember to apply your new knowledge in different situations or else you will not be able to integrate it!**

## ACTIVITY 59: Coping with provocation

The purpose of this activity is to establish your way of coping with provocation. It is closely related to criticism and conflict.

Read the following incident and answer the questions that follow:

**Incident:**
You are a teacher at a local primary school. You are sitting in your class when one of the parents, Mrs Jordan, enters without an appointment. In a very loud and angry tone of voice, she insists that you discipline one of the pupils because he is bullying her son who is also in your class. Mrs Jordan refuses to listen to your explanations, criticises your ideas and brags about her own knowledge regarding child-rearing and child psychology. She is not interested in what you have to say. At last, after you have given your views, she calls you a stupid idiot.

1. Name your physical reactions as they would have been before you studied this workbook.

   _____

   _____

2. How would you have reacted?

   _____

   _____

   _____

   _____

   _____

3. Now, with your improved knowledge and skills, how would you ensure that there are more positive consequences than negative ones? (In other words, how would you control your feelings and cope with the situation?)

   _____

   _____

   _____

   _____

   _____

   _____

   _____

## SETBACKS AND COPING WITH THEM

Everyone, at some time during their lives, experiences setbacks and disappointments. Frequently these setbacks are experienced as losses. What can be identified as setbacks?

| In the workplace: | At home/elsewhere: |
| --- | --- |
| Poor reports and negative feedback about your performance | Natural changes like the birth of a child |
| Cancellation of projects | Disasters like floods |
| Changing jobs | You experience a divorce |
| You are not promoted | You lose a loved one |
| You are retrenched | Serious family conflict |
| You are out of a job | You are involved in an armed robbery/rape/hijacking |

A considerable number of other events and situations can be included in this list, as each person experiences his life uniquely. What is a serious setback for one person is not necessarily experienced as such by another person. People react differently to setbacks. The setbacks and disappointments mentioned above give rise to negative *feelings* such as anger, depression, fear and anxiety, which may lead to negative *behaviour* like withdrawal, the use of alcohol and drugs or becoming aggressive. This behaviour affects the person's whole family and other areas of life. However, some people have the ability to restore themselves and return to the same level of functioning as before.

Various factors determine the resilience of some people, for example:

1. Individual factors like: personal capabilities, the ability to plan, cognitive skills, optimism, internal locus of control ("I am in control of my feelings"), skills to cope with stress and the ability to look for support systems and to use them.

2. Family factors: family support, warmth and caring.
3. Community factors: support systems like ministers, teachers, etc.[31]

Resilience is hampered by past unresolved and unprocessed emotional trauma. As soon as a person can admit and accept these dark times in his life, he becomes stronger and freer to cope with the new problems in his life. Then there are no old feelings which arise and demand energy.

"What lies before us and what lies behind us are tiny matters compared to what lies within us."
*Oliver Wendell Holmes*

## ACTIVITY 60: Emotional resilience

The goal of the following activity is to recognise situations in your life that may hamper your resilience.

1. Gain perspective about events in your life about which you still do not feel at ease. They may have happened a long time ago or they may have happened recently. Complete the following table.

| Event or feeling | Present in your life Yes/No | Briefly describe the events |
|---|---|---|
| Experience rejection | | |
| Experience feelings of guilt | | |
| You are intensely regretful about something | | |
| You are intensely embittered about something | | |
| You have not completed a grieving process | | |

2. What is there in your life, past or present, about which you do not want to think or talk?

3. Draw up a list of things you miss in your life, which (you think) may prevent your life from being full and happy. Which feelings do you associate with each item on your list?

_____

_____

4. Which feelings, e.g. anger, disguise the primary feelings of fear and sadness?

_____

_____

5. Are you experiencing a feeling of desperation at the thought of having to let go of issues that you have not given attention to for a long time? Explain this.

_____

_____

_____

## ACTIVITY 61: Emotional resilience: a specific situation

Answer the following questions for each situation in the previous activity which you have identified as a possible problem. Write down the answers to gain more clarity.

1. What aspect of this situation do I have to accept?

_____

_____

2. What in particular do I have to learn from this situation?

_____

_____

3. Which perspective am I ignoring? Can I look at it from a different perspective that will relieve my feelings?

_____

_____

4. What will the benefits be if I can change my perspective?

_____

_____

5. Which new skills can I develop to cope with this problem or do I have the necessary skills already?

_____

_____

6. How can I let go of the old feelings that are related to these events?

_____

_____

### Improve your resilience

You may not know whether you have these skills or not when you are confronted with a situation where you need them. Perhaps you can practise these skills by visualising and thus preparing yourself for these types of situations. These tips may improve your resilience. Practise them when you experience a situation that taxes your resilience or during visualisation:

- Become aware of your feelings and your interpretations of them. Enhance your emotional awareness.
- Don't ignore or suppress the feelings that you experience. If you are sad, express this by crying; if you are angry, punch your pillow.
- Keep your self-talk motivating and maintain a good sense of humour.
- Try as far as possible to relax.

- Get involved in physical activities, like walking, exercising, working in the garden.
- Use problem-solving techniques.
- Identify and use your support systems.
- Reconsider your goals and formulate new ones if necessary.

### Phases from a setback to a comeback

The following seven phases form part of the restoration process. Determine in which phase you find yourself in terms of setbacks you have experienced or are experiencing.

| Phases | Description | In which phase are you? |
|---|---|---|
| Phase 1: Disbelief | Short-term denial may help at this stage to protect you from strong emotions. Become aware of distorted thinking patterns and of all the feelings you experience. | |
| Phase 2: Anger | Control your feelings. Try to think constructively and do physical exercises. | |
| Phase 3: Want to turn back the clock | You have an intense wish for everything to be as it was before. Acknowledge the feelings and recognise that it is not possible to turn back the clock. Start to explore realistic and practical steps you may take. | |
| Phase 4: Depression | This is the biggest hurdle to overcome. You feel apathetic and hopeless. Use your sources of motivation and keep a record of your feelings. | |
| Phase 5: Acceptance | Your confidence is returning. Focus on your goals, needs/wishes and plan to reach them. | |
| Phase 6: Hope | Optimism is experienced once again. You feel hopeful and full of confidence. | |
| Phase 7: Positive activity | Your motivation is back and you can consciously move ahead. | |

Remember that you may return to earlier phases. This process is experienced differently by different people. You should work through each phase before going on to the next one.[32]

## ACTIVITY 62: Support systems

Name the support systems available to you in times of crisis:

1. Yourself (e.g. I find it easy to stay calm, etc.)

_____

_____

2. Your community/situation (e.g. your family, neighbours, etc.)

_____

3. Which of the above do you use most and why?

_____

_____

4. Which do you use least and why?

_____

_____

"In the depth of winter, I finally learned that there was in me an invincible summer."
*Albert Camus*

## FORGIVENESS AND THE RESTORA-TION OF BROKEN RELATIONSHIPS

To restore broken relationships, you have to take responsibility, admit your mistakes and apologise honestly. When you say you're sorry, you have to be very specific, e.g. "I am sorry that I insulted you in front of your family." Apologies from others may be accepted or rejected. You may reject an apology when it is not uttered in honesty or if it is not specific. Express your feelings; don't suppress or put them away. Forgiveness should be genuine. People find it difficult to forgive themselves and others. The nurturing of a hurtful event from the past keeps you from experiencing happiness and striving for your dreams, since you cling to the past and don't look to the future. This is a very appropriate quotation:

"By forgiving, you set someone else free, to find that you yourself were the prisoner."
*Anonymous*

Accept yourself and others as human beings. You will find it difficult to maintain positive relationships with others if you have not accepted yourself and feel good about yourself, because you radiate negative energy about yourself. Trust is to believe that others are just as acceptable as you are, not more or less. No one is perfect and we all may make mistakes. If someone honestly asks you for forgiveness, grant it and restore the relationship. If you are at fault and this is preventing you from being happy, forgive yourself. Strive to be happy – it is a conscious choice.

**Keep a watchful eye on the following irrational thoughts that keep you in the past:**

"If only I did not . . ."
"I wish I had said or done something else . . ."
"I should have reacted differently . . ."
"I am so sorry . . ."
"If only I could do it again . . ."

People need emotional strokes, which may be verbal or nonverbal, like hugs or compliments. You should be able to ask for them and you should not withhold them from others. Strokes may be accepted or rejected as well, but you should think about it carefully. You have to give strokes to yourself, as self-love enhances self-acceptance and confirms your relationships. You should not react negatively to a compliment, but positively. If someone says that they like your dress, don't react with: "Oh, it is an old dress that I bought on a sale." Rather be positive and reply: "Thank you very much, that is nice to hear."

Remember that material things or people are like sweets. They are pleasant to have, but not essential like oxygen to stay alive. If you are emotionally dependent on others, they are in control of your life/oxygen. With a single negative situation (which you may interpret wrongly), your oxygen can be cut off and you will stop breathing. Think about other people as something pleasant to have (like sweets and cake), but not essential to survive.

## ACTIVITY 63: Emotional restoration/strokes

Draw up a list of as many as possible "healing" words and deeds that you can use in your daily life to restore and build relationships. Try to apply these daily. (Examples: say your are sorry, please, thank you, I forgive you, give a hug, flower or compliment, etc.)

## ACTIVITY 64: Emotional baggage

Ask yourself what have you learnt from your parents, at school, etc. about the following (which could have led to irrational assumptions):

| | | | |
|---|---|---|---|
| Money | | About being a spouse | |
| Spirituality | | About receiving | |
| Feelings | | About giving | |
| About being a parent | | Sex | |
| Happiness | | About being a son or a daughter | |
| Work | | Alcohol | |
| About being a man | | Love | |
| About being a woman | | Religion | |
| About being a friend | | Family | |
| Communication | | Fun | |
| Specific feelings like anger, guilt, shame | | Cultural differences | |

Indicate which of the above were taught to you wrongly or not at all, and which are causing problems in you adult life. Accept that it is not your fault, but it is your **responsibility to learn the necessary skills and obtain the necessary knowledge in order to cope with the problems.** Take steps to do this. Remember that this activity is not meant to make you feel negative about your parents, teachers and important others. On the contrary, you have to make a conscious choice to leave the problems behind after you have evaluated them from an adult perspective.

## ACTIVITY 65: Self-forgiveness

The purpose of this activity is not to make you feel negative towards your parents or other people. Remember, parents are mostly well meaning. You have to gain insight into the reasons for the feelings that you find hard to let go of and you have to take steps towards processing them. Make peace with your past.

Complete the following sentences:

My mother always said: _____

My mother always said: _____

My mother always said: _____

My father always said: _____
My father always said: _____
My father always said: _____
My mother/father always looked at me in a certain way when I _____
My teacher always said: _____
My teacher always said: _____
My teacher always said: _____

How many of the above included a remark about emotions? Are they all about rejection or invalidation of your feelings? How many of them did you feel embarrassed about even though they were meant to address your behaviour (and not your feelings)?

Which emotions did you experience while thinking about these past events?
_____

Is it possible for you to forgive these people for what they did?
_____

## ACTIVITY 66: Forgiveness

1. Read an article about trauma in a magazine or newspaper. In which way could forgiveness have changed or prevented the outcome? If you were in this situation, would you have been able to forgive?

2. Put a drop of food colouring in a glass of water. Observe how the water changes colour and imagine how a grudge can colour and influence your whole body negatively.

## CHANGES AND CHOICES ABOUT YOUR LIFE SITUATIONS

We are frequently confronted with situations we feel uncertain about coping with, or just give up trying to cope with. The following activity provides you with guidelines on how to evaluate different situations and how you should react to each. Remember that it is your choice whether to look at the situation as a challenge or a threat.

The ideal is to control your problems or let them go (accept that you can't do anything about them). The art is in identifying the different situations and then deciding in which category they should be. Not all situations can be divided into one of the categories, e.g. a difficult work situation that you cannot change, but cannot let go of either. Try to accept situations without paying too high an emotional price. Remember that you have to make a conscious choice regarding what you want to change and then start changing it, although you may feel uncomfortable at first. If you wait until you feel comfortable, you will never change your behavioural patterns.

## ACTIVITY 67: Change your personal situation

Indicate on the chart which situations you cope with according to one of the four alternatives. Determine which problems have to be controlled or let go of. Plan consciously to do one of the two.

| | ACTION | INDICATE YOUR PROBLEMS/NEEDS HERE |
|---|---|---|
| X | **1. Cannot be changed, but you keep on trying.** You continually try to change things in your life which you cannot change. You spend a lot of energy on something you have no control over. | |
| ✓ | **2. "Let go" that which you cannot change.** You admit that you want to let it go. You experience no feelings of guilt about it. You forget about it. | |
| X | **3. You can change something, but you don't try either.** All things which you can change and control, but which you don't give any attention to or have given up on, are in this category. | |
| ✓ | **4. It can be changed – just do it.** All things which you can control and change. Evaluate your life carefully and start to change where possible. | |

Letting go of certain events from your past demands emotional power and the knowledge that it will be to your benefit. Emotionally it is very tiring to be reminded of things about which you can't do anything and which you can't control. Even a very insignificant event during your childhood may linger and give rise to irrational assumptions and unexplained behaviour. Examine yourself carefully to recognise your emotional baggage. Remember that letting go relates strongly to self-forgiveness and the forgiveness of others. There is a great deal of acceptance involved as well. Acceptance implies that we make peace with things as they are and frequently not as we would want them to be. As long as we believe that the world should be the way we want it to be, we will not try to cope with reality.

### Be good to yourself!

**Autosuggestion**: Say the following to yourself when you are relaxed, because your brain will ignore information that does not fit existing patterns if you are not relaxed. When you repeat the confirmations often enough to yourself, they will go to your subconscious and influence your attitude and approach to life. Repeat them when you wake up, just before you fall asleep, before and after meetings, while you are driving, etc. until they become part of you.

I am able to change my life.
I am worthy of love.
I am able to learn from previous experiences.
It is acceptable for me to make a mistake.
My past does not control my feelings.
I believe in people.
I am a good person.
I am loved.
I accept myself.
I enjoy what life gives me.
I am able to do anything.
I can learn something new daily.

**Remember:**
- Let go of the guilt of the past.
- Change negative assumptions.
- Know your own values.
- Admit that people have different values and assumptions.
- Know your own rules and decide for yourself if you want to change them.
- Acknowledge the pain of your past and then forget about it.
- Identify the value of getting rid of old anger.

## The power of the present

One's life can be divided into three periods of time. Each of them implies different feelings. This can be shown as follows:

| Past | Present | Future |
|------|---------|--------|
| Anger<br>Hurt<br>Sadness<br>Guilt | **POWER** | Worry<br>Fear<br>Anxiety |

When we tend to live too much in the past or to worry too much about the future, we may lose the present (where we have power) and as a result of this the future may be just like the past. It is only in the now where we have the power to bring about change. When you are in a situation in the present, follow these steps:

1. Observe and become aware of what is going on around you;
2. What are your alternatives (regarding the situation/need/problem)?

3. What can you learn from the alternatives?
4. What can you do differently to ensure that your future is different from your past? [33]

It is only by living fully in the present that we have the power to let go of the past and to influence the future directly by the decisions we make.

## ACTIVITY 68: "Letting go"

Write the following on a small piece of paper:
– the name of a person you love dearly;
– something you hope for or a goal you have for yourself and
– a symbol or quotation which usually helps you through difficult times.

Fold the paper as small as possible and put it into a balloon. Blow it up. Draw on the balloon the face of someone whom you must forgive or with whom you have to make peace. You could write on it a situation which troubles you and which you have to let go of. Jump on the balloon so that you use plenty of physical energy in your "letting go" action. Take the piece of paper (all that is left), read it and put it where you can look at it regularly.

"Our whole success in life consists in our ability to let go."
*Mary Yeates*

## HAPPINESS AS A CHOICE

As mentioned earlier, an emotionally intelligent person is able to cope with most negative situations. Everyone knows that in every situation there are mainly two things between which to choose: to see the situation negatively or to look at it optimistically as an opportunity for growth. Remember that the absence of negative situations and circumstances in your life does not mean that you will experience happiness. One may have an attitude of happiness notwithstanding what happens in and around you. What is important is your perspective of what happiness really is. Everyone is capable of experiencing happiness – it is not something which is selectively given to some and not to others.

Happiness is a conscious choice that you should make yourself. It is not an automatic response and no one can make the choice to be happy on your behalf. In other words, you are responsible for your own happiness. This means that you cannot expect others to make you happy and other people cannot expect you to make them happy. This removes a huge emotional burden from you and others if everyone accepts the responsibility for his/her own happiness.

It is not **what** happens which determines your life, but the **way** you cope with it. If you cope with a difficult situation with patience and care, you experience positive feelings. This is what happiness is. In each situation you can only give your best and do what you regard as the best option. Learn to let go of things which do not bring you pleasant feelings. Happiness is the knowledge that you have reached something – a feeling of triumph. It is within your reach – but only as far as thinking a new kind of thought or changing your perspectives. If you believe that you are happy, you will possibly experience happiness more easily, as this is the perspective you use to look at your life. You think constructively. You have to be willing to take risks and strive for your goals. To be happy, you have to be courageous. Get rid of all your defences and excuses.

Happiness relates to "being" and "giving" much more than to "doing" and "receiving". This means that happiness is not always directly related to what you receive (degrees/certificates) and to what you have (material possessions). Accept what you cannot change. Happiness means a lot of acceptance and it is not related to who you are, where you are, with whom you are, or what you have. If you do not accept yourself, you will not experience happiness, even though your situation may change a lot.

Happiness is related to behaviour that is governed by moral values. This means that you cannot strive for happiness at all costs and hurt people. Get involved with people and enjoy their company. It is essential to do this if you tend to get depressed. It may be necessary to delay the fulfilment of your needs to experience happiness later on.

Try to bring more humour into your life. Valuable chemicals are released in your body when you laugh. These chemicals may enhance your health and may help you to overcome depression.

Hope is closely related to happiness, as it provides energy, possibility, excitement and positive growth (to change) opportunities. Hope may indicate to you that you are not satisfied with your life as it is. Ask yourself what you hope for, what it will give you and what it will mean. Keep on asking this question until you have reached the core of your hopes (laddering). Plan consciously to reach this. Hope without action is worthless and may be destructive. It is important that you strive to bring your hope to fulfilment. Hope alone will not give rise to change and growth – it only creates unrealistic expectations that will lead to disappointment. To live purposefully is hope in action.

The following diagram indicates the **blockages** which might be between you and happiness.

| Myself | | |
| --- | --- | --- |
| ↓ | | |
| **Misconceptions** | **Preconditions** | **Assumptions** |
| What is happiness? | I have to earn happiness. | Happiness does not last long. |
| If I can have "this", I will be happy. | | |
| | ↓ | |
| | Happiness | |

## ACTIVITY 69: Recognition of negative assumptions/beliefs with regard to happiness

Complete as many of the following sentences as possible as you have identified them in yourself. (E.g. to be happy, I must lose weight.)

To be happy, I must

_____

To be happy, I must

_____

To be happy, I must

_____

To be happy, I must

_____

To be happy, I must

_____

## ACTIVITY 70: Incomplete sentences about happiness

This activity is aimed at giving you more insight into your viewpoint on happiness:

1. Happiness is

_____

_____

2. I feel happy when

_____

_____

3. The feelings which I experience when I feel happy are

_____

_____

_____

4. When I am happy I do the following

_____

_____

_____

5. I always thought happiness was

_____

_____

_____

6. I realise now that happiness is

_____

_____

_____

7. To experience more happiness, I will

_____

_____

_____

8. Feelings of happiness have to be

_____

9. I am at my happiest when

_____

10. My happiness makes other people

_____

11. Other people's happiness makes me

_____

## ACTIVITY 71: Situations in which I experience happiness

Write down as many things as possible that enhance your happiness/joy/pleasure. It may be doing something, e.g. having a pizza, picking flowers, going to the movies, etc. Keep this list on hand and read through it often. You can add new things as well. When you feel down, read the list and do some of the things you have described. (Remember that happiness is not necessarily situation-bound, it is rather an inner state of mind.) **Prolong your happy moments!**

## SUMMARY

Intense emotional situations (such as when you are criticised) demand a lot of your self-control and coping strategies. If you usually have problems coping with these situations, go carefully through this chapter again. Practise your new knowledge and skills in other similar situations. Remember that it may be difficult for you at first to break old behavioural patterns because they are such an integral part of yourself. When you practise the new skills and apply them to social situations, where applicable, they will become part of your behaviour.

Try purposefully to change and control what you can in your life. Strive to complete and let go of everything that is no longer in your interest. Restore those relationships that are valuable to you, and leave emotional baggage behind. Remember that the past has no control over you, except what you permit it to have. Make the decision to be happy and start living as if it were already true!

In the last chapter we will focus on the identification of areas where you want to change and how to do it. It is in this chapter where you commit yourself to change if necessary.

# CHAPTER 8
## where do I go from here?

At the beginning of the book we said that the start of a process of change is to take responsibility for your own life and happiness, and whether or not to start is your choice. Part of this process is to determine the skills and traits you already have which lead to positive feelings and behaviour. You can do this with the help of your new knowledge about yourself and your internal functioning. When you become aware of the skills you already have, you facilitate your growth and enhance your self-worth. Therefore it is important to realise that you have a foundation for further growth and that it is not necessary to change everything. You already have certain special qualities and skills, because everything you have done until now was not necessarily wrong. We frequently focus on what we cannot do and what we do "incorrectly" instead of focusing on what we have and are able to do. The goal of the following activity is to evaluate yourself and to summarise what you have already, and on which you must continue building.

## ACTIVITY 72: Your present skills

Complete the following:

1. Which of your values as they are now or as they were before you studied this workbook result in positive feelings?

2. Which of your needs have been and are being satisfied?

3. Do you use your journal and are you planning purposefully to satisfy your needs?

4. Which of your thought patterns/assumptions have given you the power to cope positively with your life in the past?

5. Which behaviour/reaction leads to positive results for you?

6. Which goals have you achieved in the past?

7. Which skills do you already have that facilitate your relationship with yourself and others?

8. Other (e.g. positive traits)

Now you know what you already have. By combining this with what you have learnt in the preceding chapters of this book, you should see a clear picture of the things you want to change and the skills you want to learn. We said at the beginning of the book that it is not easy to change and that you may experience resistance. Is this how you feel at the moment? You will be guided through your fears about change in the rest of this chapter. Remember that one usually goes through four phases before one is able to change: denial, resistance, rediscovery and commitment.

## WHY CHANGE?

If there is one thing we can be certain about, it is the fact that every one of us will go through a series of changes during our lifetime and that we will have to adapt to them. We often fail to change as a result of the disguised benefits of staying the way we are (we do not admit this to ourselves). We would rather stay in an uncomfortable known situation than change to a more comfortable, but uncertain, situation.

The situations/changes may be the following:

- starting school;
- starting work;
- changing work circumstances;
- changing jobs;
- being retrenched;
- stopping work (e.g. as a result of the birth of a child);
- a change in your financial position;
- becoming a housewife after years of working outside the home;
- the birth of a child;
- divorce;
- a second marriage;
- relocating;
- changing health situation;
- the death of a loved one;
- emigration;
- going on pension, etc.

If you prepare yourself for change during your lifetime and accept the idea, it will be easier for you to adapt. While it is true that people are highly adaptable, change demands energy and people often choose to stay in the same circumstances if possible.

Change and adaptation may hold lots of uncertainty and cannot always be planned in detail beforehand. Your feelings about change and your experience of the process of change will depend to a large extent on your viewpoint (perspective). If you believe that you will not adapt easily to change, any changing process will be difficult for you. On the other hand, if you believe that change is a kind of adventure which makes life more interesting, you will find it easier to adapt and you will experience more positive feelings.

## ACTIVITY 73: Change

Do the following activity to determine your viewpoint/attitude about change:

1. What does change mean to you (what is your perspective)?
   _____
   _____
   _____

2. Identify your negative/irrational assumptions regarding change (e.g. "I don't like change" or "I do not adapt easily").
   _____
   _____
   _____

3. Rephrase the sentence above so that it contains more constructive assumptions.
   _____
   _____
   _____
   _____

4. What do you want to change as a result of your enhanced knowledge and skills which you can do easily?
   _____
   _____
   _____

5. What do you want most to change?
   _____
   _____
   _____

6. What is the greatest fear/hurdle which you have to overcome before you can start to change?
   _____
   _____
   _____
   _____

## ACTIVITY 74: Resistance to change

The purpose of this activity is to point out how much uneasiness a simple change can cause, but that it is possible to make changes. Take a pen and a clean sheet of paper. Draw anything you can think of which you see regularly at home or in the office. Do this drawing with the hand you usually do not write with. Give the paper to a friend without saying what it is and ask him to write down the name of the object on the same piece of paper.

Ask yourself the following questions:

* Did your friend identify the object correctly?

_____

* How did you feel while writing with the "wrong" hand?

_____

* Did you feel unsure about whether or not your friend would identify the object correctly?

_____

* Did you experience resistance/were you uncomfortable by making such a simple change?

_____

* How can you overcome resistance to change?

_____

It is necessary to identify your ideals/dreams in order to facilitate your adaptation to change and to make change happen (being proactive rather than reactive, where you just react to what happens to you). To be able to reach your ideals, you have to formulate clear goals, remembering that ideals/dreams may not always be great successes. Some examples are:

* to stop smoking;
* to lose weight;
* to renovate your home;
* to start living in a more health-conscious way.

Your list may include things like the following:
* to organise your cupboards;
* to sort the incoming mail;
* to do the dishes immediately after a meal;
* to keep up with your exercise programme.

The clearer the picture of what you want to attain, the easier it will be for you to formulate realistic goals.

In the next section we focus on the formulation of goals in general. Goals regarding your growth as a result of this workbook will be formulated in Activity 79.

## GOAL-SETTING

Goals are important as they force us to look carefully at life and to decide what is important to us. They motivate us and keep us focused so we don't follow other pathways impulsively. By identifying our goals, our dreams take on a more realistic and attainable form. When we achieve our goals we experience a feeling of satisfaction which enhances our self-worth. Your knowledge, skills, mood and readiness play a role in your goal-setting.

### Determine your goals

Keep the following in mind when determining your goals:

* Goals may be specific, e.g. with regard to daily tasks.
* They may be long term, e.g. to manage your time or to give more support and strokes to other people. Remember that your short-term goals motivate you, and when you reach them, you will feel more encouraged to work on your long-term goals. Goals have to be challenging, but achievable,

realistic and within a certain time frame. Visualise a future event, feeling or mood as a possible goal and write it down as follows: "My goal is to . . . on . . . (date). I will know that I am on my way if . . . To reach this goal, I will . . . (plan of action) from . . . (date)."

- Plan specific tasks with time limits in order to achieve the goal. If you want to achieve the goal within a year, revise it every three months. Am I making any progress?
- Medium-term goals are those you want to reach on your way to the long-term one. These have to be measurable, realistic, feasible and achievable as well. Your long-term goal is to achieve something within three years. After that time you can formulate another new long-term goal.
- Goals may be formulated according to the roles you have to fulfil, e.g. your role as father, spouse, manager, church leader, etc. Remember that you do not live in isolation but in relation to others. You have to formulate your goals so that other people are kept in mind.
- Goals may be changed and adapted. Don't stick to your goals rigidly if they don't fit your lifestyle or planning any more. If you experience a strong gut feeling about something, explore the feasibility of it and do it. You can always return to your original goals.

"Prayer is our way of talking to God. Intuition is God's way of talking to us."
*Mike Lipkin*

## ACTIVITY 75: To help with goal-setting

By completing the following sentences you will become aware of what you enjoy doing and what you have to plan for in your journal to give attention to your own needs.

1. I would like to

   _____

   again.

2. I would like to

   _____

   at least once.

3. It would be nice to

   _____

   more often.

4. I have to

   _____

   soon.

5. Before the end of the year, I want to

   _____

6. It would be very nice to

   _____

   just once more.

7. I would like to

   _____

   within the next two weeks.

8. Something I would like to achieve in my life is

   _____

9. I would like to

   _____

   once a day.

10. It would be good for me to

    _____

    at least once a week.

11. I want to

    _____

    for the people close to me.

## ACTIVITY 76: Goals

The following activity enables you to think differently (bigger) than your immediate situation/environment. It clarifies your goals.

1. Draw up a list of things you would have done had you had unlimited time and resources (like money).

   _____

   _____

   _____

What can you do about it now?

_____

_____

_____

_____

_____

_____

2. Compile a list of what you think the world needs.

_____

_____

_____

Set yourself one goal to contribute to the world.

_____

_____

_____

_____

_____

_____

"Take short steps. A lot of people fail because they take too big a step quickly."
_Zig Ziglar_

## Personal mission statement

Try to write your own philosophy of life or mission statement in which you declare your goals. Your mission statement should contain the values and assumptions on which you base your life; the principles which guide you. It contains aspects like: What is the purpose of your life? What gives you purpose and meaning? What do you want to leave your loved ones? What do you want to be and do? You may write your statement in terms of the different aspects of yourself (i.e. physical, psychological, spiritual, etc.) and/or in terms of the roles you play in your daily life.

Writing your own mission statement is one of the most important steps you can take in your life. Your philosophy should be like a compass, which indicates to you that you are on the right track and when you get distracted from your goals.

## ACTIVITY 77: Mission statement

In order to write your own mission statement, imagine yourself being at your own funeral.[34] What would you like the people who are there to say about you? For example: "He was a loyal friend" or "She loved children." Include in your mission statement the type of person you want to be as well as the achievements/performances for which you have to strive. Write these down as clearly as possible, e.g. "I will always try to be a loyal friend" or "I always do my best at work." You can also add reminders to yourself, such as "Listen before you speak" or "Consider all viewpoints before coming to a conclusion."

_____

_____

_____

_____

## ACTIVITY 78: Values and mission

Choose one value that is most important to you (e.g. loyalty). Write it down on a piece of paper and put it in your purse or stick it to a mirror/fridge where you can see it frequently. Make sure that you do something to confirm this value at least once a day. By doing this activity, you start to live according to your mission.

"Unless you try to do something beyond what you have mastered, you will never grow."
_John Beecher_

You have to decide what you want to keep in your life and what you want to change. Ask yourself the following questions: Which of my behaviours or attitudes do I want to change, e.g. my viewpoint of life or my perspectives? Do my present values and assumptions give rise to unmet needs and negative feelings?

What are my unmet needs? Can I do anything about them? How did I cope with my feelings in the past and how do I want to cope with them in the future? Do I need to be more self-assertive and take myself into account? How did I communicate in the past? Do I want to change that? Use visualisation (see p. 101) to determine your goals. Remember not to visualise only one goal, but others in the same direction as well. This means that you will have more options to reach your goals in other (possibly similar) ways.

## ACTIVITY 79: Commitment to changing thinking patterns and behaviour

The purpose of this activity is to summarise your identified growth areas and to construct a framework for your future personal growth. Please give special attention to this activity. (Use all the information from the previous activities.)

Start now by making a conscious choice that you want to change – commit yourself to it!

### 1. Values:
Write down ten of the most important values that you want to pursue and which will guide your life.

| | |
|---|---|
| 1. E.g. I want to achieve independence and competence in my work | 6. |
| 2. | 7. |
| 3. | 8. |
| 4. | 9. |
| 5. | 10. |

### 2. Needs
Write down your ten most important needs that you have to give attention to.

| | |
|---|---|
| 1. E.g. Hard work/independence at work | 6. |
| 2. | 7. |
| 3. | 8. |
| 4. | 9. |
| 5. | 10. |

## 3. Assumptions/convictions/prejudices

Write down ten alternative assumptions that you have to believe in from now on and with which you have to experiment.

| | |
|---|---|
| 1. E.g. If I really want to, I can improve my competence and performance at work. | 6. |
| 2. | 7. |
| 3. | 8. |
| 4. | 9. |
| 5. | 10. |

## 4. Goals

Formulate at least ten goals regarding your needs and assumptions. Arrange the goals according to priority.

| | |
|---|---|
| 1. E.g. To be competent. | 6. |
| 2. | 7. |
| 3. | 8. |
| 4. | 9. |
| 5. | 10. |

## 5. Tasks and possible hurdles

Draw up a list of tasks that have to be done and possible hurdles that have to be overcome in order to reach the goals. Give each task a deadline, and evaluate later whether it has been reached or not.

| Tasks | Deadline | Has it been reached or not? |
|---|---|---|
| 1. E.g. Attend a computer course. Determine the best date for the course. | End of the year. | |
| 2. | | |
| 3. | | |
| 4. | | |
| 5. | | |
| 6. | | |

| Tasks | Deadline | Has it been reached or not? |
|-------|----------|------------------------------|
| 7. | | |
| 8. | | |
| 9. | | |
| 10. | | |

**Important:** In determining these tasks, you should formulate them in terms of practical things which you have to do.

The following aspects are important to strengthen and integrate the new knowledge and skills:

- Start making your self-talk constructive and believe in what you say to yourself.
- Sensory experiences and feedback are important. How will my senses tell me when I have reached my goals? What will I feel, hear, see, etc. For example, if I stop smoking, I will feel healthier, will not smell of smoke, etc.
- Visualise how you will master your new skills and reach your goals.
- Try to achieve small successes. Generate a small success each day that will encourage you to keep to your new lifestyle.
- Repetition is very important in the integration of any new patterns. Repeat your new goals frequently to yourself.

Write down the reinforcements which you want to use with regard to your specific goals in the next chart. Be as specific as possible, so that you can start from today!

| Self-talk | Sensory confirmations | Visualisation | Small successes |
|-----------|----------------------|---------------|-----------------|
| 1. I can do this work already. | I can see that my work is done. | How I work competently. | Each task I can do on my own. |
| 2. | | | |
| 3. | | | |
| 4. | | | |
| 5. | | | |
| 6. | | | |
| 7. | | | |
| 8. | | | |
| 9. | | | |
| 10. | | | |

## ACTIVITY 80: Goals postcard

After you have formulated your goals and set yourself deadlines, do the following to have a visual reminder of your resolutions and to motivate you: Take a postcard and address it to yourself. Congratulate yourself on reaching your first goals as if you had reached them already. Give it to your best friend and ask her to mail it to you within six weeks.

Example: Dear Sally, Congratulations! I see you have already lost seven kilograms. You have succeeded in using emotional control in ten situations. I am proud of you. Sally.

Remember to address it to yourself. Ask the same friend to phone you after three and eight weeks to ask about your success in reaching your goals.

## ACTIVITY 81: Personal growth

The following activity will guide you to assess the changes and growth which have taken place in yourself in a creative way. This will help you to get a realistic view of your changes and growth and may also motivate you to grow further towards reaching your potential.

Put a clean sheet of paper in a tray. Take six containers and put each of the following into one of them: sand, sugar, red, green and yellow jelly and black cocoa. Use these to make a picture of your life. You may form symbols, colours, lines, etc. – anything which resembles the growth process up to that moment in your life. Take a photograph of this and look at it regularly. Evaluate where you have been and where you are now. What did you learn from your experiences?

You can also make/draw a second picture of your life as you want it to be at the end of the process. Take a photograph of it and compare the two pictures to recognise new goals.

## SELF-MOTIVATION

What is motivation? Motivation means that you spend energy on reaching a certain goal. The greater your passion/desire to reach a certain goal, the more motivated you will be and the more energy you will use. This enhances the probability that you will reach your goal. Why is it important that you are able to motivate yourself? People who can motivate themselves can be proactive in making things happen and establishing change. They are positive about life and are not easily discouraged by problems.

On the other hand, people who cannot motivate themselves are helpless victims who only react to what happens to them. They tend to get depressed and give up when their first try is not successful. If you are able to motivate yourself at work, you need less supervision, you are absent less frequently and you are more productive and creative.

If you visualise what you want to achieve, you improve your motivation to work at it.

### Sources of motivation [35]

You yourself are the most powerful source of motivation. Your thoughts have to be encouraging and you have to be able to visualise how you will successfully reach your goal. Learn to take action and transform it into the energy you need. When you feel that your energy levels are low, start moving! Listen to lively music and feel how your energy increases. Divide the task at hand into smaller, easy-to-reach pieces.

Friends, family and colleagues may be sources of motivation. They must be trustworthy, available and suited for the purpose, which means that they themselves should be motivated. You have to inform them about your goals and you can use their objectivity. They will possibly recognise your distorted thinking and can give you more clarity. You have to be available for them as well. Get yourself an emotional mentor who is able to motivate and inspire you.

It is your responsibility to arrange your environment (office/home) so that it is healthy and organised. There should be enough fresh air and sunlight with no disturbing odours, noise or colours. You might like to arrange photos and notes with encouraging quotations in your working environment. In the light of the above, what can you do to make your environment more supporting and motivational?

Self-motivation relates to levels of stress, the challenges associated with certain tasks and the skills you already have. If you experience too much stress, your goal is not challenging enough or you do not have the skills to fulfil it, you will find it difficult to motivate yourself. A certain amount of stress is necessary before you decide to change. If the goal or proposed change is challenging enough and you have the skills to succeed, you will be motivated to do so.

In the light of the above, you have to determine your levels of stress and what kind of challenge it is for you to change. Having worked through this workbook and practised the different skills, you should be able to bring about the necessary changes.

*"To achieve personal fulfilment, you must be prepared to take action toward your goal. When you do, you find that all sorts of extraordinary things may begin to happen."*
*Anonymous*

## SUMMARY

This book is a guide to reaching those parts of your humanity which are often neglected in society's striving towards physical and intellectual stimulation/ development. With the (re)discovery of your "truth" (regarding your values, assumptions and needs) you take the first step towards becoming the person you can be. By positively and constructively programming your brain and eliminating hampering assumptions, you are another step closer to reaching optimal growth. By beginning to question your "truth" (viewpoint of life) and realising that it may differ from those of other people, you enable yourself to see the world with different, new eyes. What a joyful exploration! It is liberating to find that things may be different from what you thought they were and should be. Open your mind to other possibilities and other ways of doing things. Remember that you always have a choice about how you look at and interpret events. Your attitude is the determining factor in how you experience your environment, and you may choose whether you want to look at it positively or negatively.

It is easier for you to establish and maintain social relationships when you realise that people are unique regarding their thoughts, feelings and behaviour. Forgive people who have hurt you. Be willing to forgive yourself as well. A person is part of a social system and you cannot cut yourself off from it. The emotionally intelligent person has good relationships with others and compassion for his fellow man that is clear from his behaviour.

Accepting what you cannot change is an important step. Accepting yourself and others paves the way to happiness and fulfilment. There is little that does so much harm as an obstinate clinging to something which you can't do anything about. It is nearly impossible to experience happiness if you don't accept yourself and your circumstances. However, this acceptance does not mean that you wait passively and submissively for life to happen to you. Instead, it is an active experiencing of your situation and an intervention whenever you can change something.

Change is a process that can be practised step by step over some time – it is only in this way that change becomes part of your new lifestyle. The process starts with a conscious choice to take responsibility for your own thoughts, feelings and behaviour. You are the only person who can make a difference to you own life. The control is inside you, although external sources can strengthen and support the process. You are responsible for identifying your mission, as well as the values and priorities with which you want to guide your life. Only then will you be able, with the end in mind, to start to plan the tasks which will make your life more purposeful and fulfilled. Identify that which you already have and build on it, so that your fulfilment happens so much sooner. Remember that you may make mistakes in the process of growth. If you always do what you can do, you may never make a mistake, but neither will you grow. This changing process is part of growth and the taking of risks.

Your motivation for change and growth depends on the level of stress you experience in your present situation. Are you satisfied with it as it is? If you practise the new skills as described in the workbook, you may be able to apply them successfully. The last part of motivation depends on the challenge it poses to you. We want to challenge you to change that which you can with eagerness and power, to prevent this book from becoming just another book on your shelf. It is our deepest wish that everyone who reads and uses this book may be blessed with a joyous, constructive attitude and fulfilling relationships with others.

You are capable of living your mission as a result of the unlimited power and potential of your brain. You can be the best "YOU", as you have already taken the first steps!

# ACTIVITY 82: Commitment to growth and self-improvement

**COMMITMENT TO GROWTH AND SELF-IMPROVEMENT**

I, _____, HEREBY UNDERTAKE IN THE FUTURE TO UTILISE THE KNOWLEDGE AND SKILLS WHICH I HAVE ACQUIRED WHILE STUDYING THE WORK-BOOK FOR MY OWN BENEFIT AND FOR THE BENEFIT OF THOSE AROUND ME.

IN PARTICULAR I WANT TO BRING ABOUT AN IMPROVEMENT IN MY BEHAVIOUR AND WITHIN MYSELF WITH REGARD TO:

1. _____

2. _____

3. _____

4. _____

5. _____

I ACKNOWLEDGE THAT I SIGN THIS UNDERTAKING OF MY OWN FREE WILL AND THAT I WILL DO EVERYTHING IN MY POWER TO STICK TO IT.

_____
SIGNATURE

_____
DATE

# ANSWERS: Activities

ACTIVITY 5: Identify feelings

The following feelings could have been identified:

**1. Facial expressions:**

1. Liberated, exuberant, ecstatic, excited, happy, jubilant, hysterical, free.
2. Amused, inquisitive, happy, doubting, unsure, waiting, interested.
3. Dismayed, unbelieving, bewildered, exhausted, tired, overexerted, dejected, frustrated, overwhelmed, regretful.
4. Neglected, dejected, depressed, worried, afraid, angry, sad, unhappy, sorry.
5. Surprised, startled, happy, excited, somewhat shocked, peaceful, believing.
6. Miserable, abused, disapproving, contemptuous, disillusioned, frustrated, impatient, bitter, misused, obstinate, moody.

**2. Nonverbal communication:**

1. Dejected, depressed, frustrated, sad, unhappy.
2. Satisfied, happy, fulfilled, smug.
3. Upset, angry, hysterical, frustrated, hateful.
4. Successful, satisfied, smug, happy, self-confident.
5. Rested, happy, satisfied, safe, self-confident.
6. Sad, neglected, unhappy, safe, loving, loved.

**3. Art:**

1. Anxious, paranoid, threatened, cornered, panic-stricken, afraid, powerless, hopeless, bewildered.
2. Excited, cheerful, happy, afraid, cornered, anxious, undecided.
3. Cold, insensitive, trapped, undecided, uninvolved, negative, aggressive, apathetic, confused, planned, logical, organised, purposeful, determined.
4. Happy, satisfied, balanced, optimistic, calm, motivated, thankful, hopeful, courageous, fulfilled, loved.
5. Depressed, confused, hurt, betrayed, cheated, cornered, unhappy, powerless, aggressive, murderous, vindictive, frustrated.
6. Happy, satisfied, calm, somewhat tense, hopeless, unsure, determined, optimistic, impulsive, undecided.

**4. Stories:**

1. Depressed, guilty, frustrated, relieved, tired, hopeless, exhausted.
2. Determined, calm, accepting, frustrated, relieved, satisfied.
3. Accepting, happy, fulfilled, satisfied, resigned, in control, thankful.
4. Hopeful, excited, uncertain, afraid, inferior, undecided, restless, cautious.

**5. Music:**

1. Happy, satisfied, cheerful, longing.
2. Anxious, threatened, afraid, depressed, discouraged.
3. Optimistic, full of life, motivated, excited, determined.
4. Sadness, uncertainty, trust, confidence, acceptance.
5. Excited, optimistic, happy, boisterous, exultant.

ACTIVITY 12: To divide feelings according to intensity, primary and secondary feelings, and the roles you fulfil

Here are five examples of possible divisions you could have made after reading the list of feeling words:

| FEELING | MODERATE | STRONG | VERY STRONG |
|---|---|---|---|
| Happy | Feeling good | Happy | Elated |
| Depressed | Disappointed | Pessimistic | Hopeless |
| Inadequate | Unsure | Incapable | Worthless |
| Afraid | Careful | Fearful | Anxious |
| Guilty | Regretful | Ashamed | Humiliated |

Try to identify a few primary and secondary feelings.

| PRIMARY FEELINGS | SECONDARY FEELINGS |
|---|---|
| Hurt as a result of an insult | Anger, aggression |
| Unmet emotional need (UEN): value as a person | |
| Lonely | Unhappy, unfulfilled, depressed |
| UEN (unmet emotional need): friendship, companionship | |
| Neglected | Angry, unappreciated |
| UEN: appreciation, recognition | |
| Rejected, hopeless, undecided | Depressed |
| UEN: need for direction, aim, task | |
| Appreciated, peaceful, successful | Happy |

Identify the roles you are involved with, e.g. spouse, breadwinner, house-wife, mother/father, son/daughter, church leader, etc. and identify the feelings associated with each role.

| ROLES | FEELINGS |
|---|---|
| Employee | Proud, adequate, rebellious, afraid. |
| Mother | Thankful, unappreciated, neglected. |
| Spouse | Envious, loved, appreciated, recognised. |
| Church member | Frustrated, thankful, faithful. |

ACTIVITY 13: Do you understand feelings?

1. Indicated below on a scale of 1-5 are how effective the following reactions would be in the situation described, where 1 equals totally ineffective, and 5 very effective.

**A. SITUATION**
One of your friends phones to tell you some extremely good news about himself that he has just received.

**REACTION**
(a) Congratulate him on the news.

| 1 | 2 | 3 | 4 | x |
|---|---|---|---|---|

(b) Ask him if he really deserved it.

| x | 2 | 3 | 4 | 5 |
|---|---|---|---|---|

(c) Invite him over to listen to some music.

| x | 2 | 3 | 4 | 5 |
|---|---|---|---|---|

(d) Inquire whether there is anything with which you can assist him.

| x | 2 | 3 | 4 | 5 |
|---|---|---|---|---|

(e) Enjoy the moment with your friend.

| 1 | 2 | 3 | 4 | x |
|---|---|---|---|---|

**B. SITUATION**
One of your colleagues looks upset. He asks you to go with him for a walk in the park. After a while he says that he would like to talk to you about his relationship with a married woman.

**REACTION**
(a) Ask him about his feelings to enhance your understanding of the situation. Offer your assistance with no pressure from you.

| 1 | 2 | 3 | x | 5 |
|---|---|---|---|---|

(b) Entice him into giving information about why he got involved with this woman. Try to suggest what he should do.

| x | 2 | 3 | 4 | 5 |
|---|---|---|---|---|

(c) Change the subject and say that it is inappropriate for him to discuss it with you.

| x | 2 | 3 | 4 | 5 |
|---|---|---|---|---|

(d) Tell him that you were in the same position and that you overcame it with the help of a therapist.

| 1 | 2 | 3 | 4 | x |
|---|---|---|---|---|

**C. SITUATION**
A friend phones and informs you that she has just received confirmation that she is terminally ill with lung cancer. She says that she is worried about her children.

**REACTION**
(a) Show sympathy and tell her that you know someone else in the same situation to whom you can introduce her.

| x | 2 | 3 | 4 | 5 |
|---|---|---|---|---|

(b) There is nothing that you can do to change the situation, so distract her or change the subject.

| x | 2 | 3 | 4 | 5 |
|---|---|---|---|---|

(c) Tell her that you feel extremely sorry for her. Ask her to tell you what is happening and how she feels about it.

| 1 | 2 | 3 | x | 5 |
|---|---|---|---|---|

(d) Discuss her worries and her fears. Talk to her about what it means to her and how others coped with similar situations.

| 1 | 2 | 3 | 4 | x |
|---|---|---|---|---|

2. Here it is indicated which of the actions/reactions mentioned below are **the best to cope with emotions.**

**A. SITUATION**
You have just heard that 50% of your firm's staff are going to suffer a drastic reduction in salary as a result of a reduced working week. The final decision regarding which 50% it is going to be will be taken in a month's time.

**REACTION**
(a) You know the situation is pending. As a final decision has still to be taken, you decide not to worry about it.

| 1 | 2 | x | 4 | 5 |
|---|---|---|---|---|

(b) Phone a friend and discuss the situation, hoping that he will make you feel better.

| 1 | 2 | 3 | 4 | x |
|---|---|---|---|---|

(c) Discuss it with friends and let them help you find a solution.

| 1 | 2 | 3 | x | 5 |
|---|---|---|---|---|

(d) You are too shocked to talk about it.

| 1 | x | 3 | 4 | 5 |
|---|---|---|---|---|

**B. SITUATION**
You find a cigarette in your child's pocket. When you confront him with it, he denies that he has been smoking. As his clothes smell of smoke, you confine him to the house for a month. Later you discover that he was telling the truth.

**REACTION**
(a) Console yourself with the fact that parents sometimes make mistakes and leave it at that.

| x | 2 | 3 | 4 | 5 |
|---|---|---|---|---|

(b) Tell your child that you made a mistake, even though your intentions were good. Explain why you feel so strongly about it and apologise. Discuss how you will avoid similar situations in future.

| 1 | 2 | 3 | 4 | x |
|---|---|---|---|---|

(c) Apologise, tell him that you are prepared to make amends and that you will consent to a reasonable request from him.

| 1 | 2 | 3 | x | 5 |
|---|---|---|---|---|

## 3. THE USE OF EMOTIONS

(a) The words which show you what you might have experienced when visualising feelings of jealousy are indicated on the scale below.

| Warm | | | x | | Cold |
|------|---|---|---|---|------|
| Dark | | x | | | Light |
| Low | x | | | | High |
| Orange | | | x | | Blue |
| Fast | | | | x | Slow |
| Sharp | | | | x | Blunt |
| Happy | | | x | | Unhappy |
| Good | | | | x | Bad |
| Sweet | | | x | | Sour |
| Yellow | | | x | | Purple |

(b) Possible emotions which you may experience after a very capable colleague at work pays you an unexpected compliment are indicated below.

| Comfortable | |
|-------------|---|
| Calm | |
| Guilty | |
| Optimistic | x |
| Imaginative | |
| Proud | x |
| Surprised | x |
| Trusting | |
| Energetic | x |
| Sceptical | |

## 4. UNDERSTAND EMOTIONS

Emotions can be understood on different levels and in different ways. Here it is indicated with an appropriate example whether the following are true or untrue.

(a) Emotions are sometimes simple and sometimes complex, as one emotion can be a combination of two or more feelings.

| True | Untrue |
|------|--------|
| x | |

Example: Anger = hurt and disappointment.

(b) Emotions can progressively intensify.

| True | Untrue |
|------|--------|
| x | |

Example: Unhappy – sad – depressed.

(c) Two people can interpret the same emotion differently and react to it differently.

| True | Untrue |
|------|--------|
| x | |

Example: Both experience disappointment – one cries and the other becomes angry.

(d) The results of the expression of one emotion (e.g. anger), can lead to another feeling.

| True | Untrue |
|------|--------|
| x | |

Example: If a person expresses his anger inappropriately, he may feel disappointment and frustrated afterwards.

## ACTIVITY 17: Assumptions

Your interpretations regarding situations/events are strongly influenced by the assumptions/convictions that you have. Irrational assumptions give rise to negative interpretations. The fewer irrational assumptions you have, the more energy you will have to enjoy yourself and your friends. Irrational assumptions are learnt early in life. They are like a bad habit that can be unlearnt.

Here you can see which assumptions are rational and which are irrational.

**Irrational** 1. Everybody must always like me, love me and approve of my actions otherwise I feel absolutely miserable and totally useless.

**Rational** 2. It would be pleasant if everybody liked me, but I can survive without the approval of most people. It is only the approval of close friends and people with "power" over me (like my employer) about which I should be concerned.

**Irrational** 3. I have to be perfect and competent in all respects before I will regard myself as worth something.

**Rational** 4. My personal values do not depend on how perfect or competent I am. Although I try to be as competent as possible, I am a valuable person irrespective of how well I do things.

**Irrational** 5. People who are bad, like myself, should be blamed and punished to prevent them from doing bad things in future.

**Rational** 6. It is important not to repeat the same mistakes in future. I need not blame or punish myself for what happened in the past.

**Irrational** 7. It is a total catastrophe and so bad that I cannot bear it if things are not the way I want them to be.

**Rational** 8. There is no reason why the world should be the way I want it to be. It is important to cope with life as it is. I should not complain about the fact that things are not just or the way I want them to be.

**Irrational** 9. If there is a possibility that something really bad may happen, I will constantly think about it as if it is indeed going to happen.

**Rational** 10. I will do my best to avoid future unpleasantness. Thereafter I will not concern myself about anything. I refuse to be frightened by the question: "What if it happens?"

**Irrational** 11. It is easier to avoid problems and the responsibility they entail than to cope with them.

**Rational** 12. In the long run it is easier/better to cope with problems and the responsibility they entail than to avoid them.

**Irrational** 13. I need someone stronger than myself to rely on.

**Rational** 14. I am strong enough to rely on myself.

**Irrational** 15. I have been like this since childhood and I can't change.

**Rational** 16. I can change myself at any stage during my life when I decide that it is in my interest to do so.

**Irrational** 17. I should get miserable and depressed when other people have problems.

**Rational** 18. To help other people and to have empathy with them does not mean that I should get depressed about it or get involved in their problems. How can I help them if I am depressed myself?

**Irrational** 19. It is bad and unbearable if I have to do things that I do not want or like to do.

**Rational** 20. I will not allow things that I cannot change to upset me.

### ACTIVITY 21: To identify feelings, values, assumptions and needs from events which caused negative feelings

1. Possible feelings which the person could have experienced:

    Disappointment
    Humiliation
    Anger
    Cheated
    Frustration
    Jealousy

2. Possible values of the person:

    Recognition
    Acceptance
    Approval
    Appreciation
    Fairness

3. Possible unfulfilled needs:

    Status
    Competence
    Success
    Respect

4. Possible irrational beliefs:

    If you work hard at something, it is impossible for it not to be accepted.
    If my presentation is not well accepted, the problem is with the person and not my work.
    If my boss does not accept my work, he does not accept me as a person.

### ACTIVITY 41: What price do I pay?

Below are descriptions of the price that I pay (have paid) for poor self-acceptance, a lack of confidence, self-assertiveness and/or poorly defined boundaries.

**1. At work:** My boss treats me badly and gives me too much work to do. Too little self-confidence cost me a promotion. My poor self-image makes me quiet and withdrawn at work and I don't offer my opinions. People do not know that I have good answers to their problems and think that I am inexperienced/stupid.

**2. With friends:** I have few or no friends as a result of my poor self-acceptance and little self-confidence. I have a need for more social interaction. I always go along with my friends and never give my opinion because I am unassertive. They lead me astray at times because I cannot say "no".

**3. In my love life:** I have lost potentially good marriage partners as a result of my poor self-acceptance and lack of self-confidence. My love life is poor because I cannot be spontaneous. I am always worried about how I look and what he/she thinks of me. Lack of self-assertiveness means that I always follow my partner's lead and never make any suggestions. I always follow his/her suggestions because I cannot say what I want to say.

**4. In my education/choice of career:** If I had more self-confidence and better self-acceptance I would have studied something else or I would have chosen a different career. Maybe I would have worked with people instead of spending all day in front of the computer. If I had been more self-assertive, people would not have influenced me in my choice of career and I could have chosen something I would have liked more.

# RECOMMENDED BOOKS

The list mainly includes popular science books in order to be accessible to the reader.

Arterburn, Stephen and Neal, Connie. 1997. *The emotional freedom workbook*. Thomas Nelson Publications.

Bakus, William. 1994. *Learning to tell myself the truth*. Bethany House Publishers.
Birch, Cathy. 1999. *Asserting yourself*. How To Books.
Butler, Gillian and Hope, Tony. 1995. *Managing your mind. The mental fitness guide*. Oxford University Press.

Cairnes, Margot. 1998. *Approaching the corporate heart*. Simon & Schuster.
Carnegie, Dale. 1986. *Hoe om kommer te verdryf en te begin leef*. Human & Rousseau.
Cloud, Dr Henry and Townsend, Dr John. 1992. *Boundaries*. Zondervan Publishing House.
Coetzee, Annie. 1998. *Emosioneel intelligent – Jy!* J.P. van der Walt.
Coetzee, Annie. 1997. *Kreatief – Jy!* J.P. van der Walt.
Cooper, Robert K. and Sawaf, Ayman. 1996. *Executive EQ*. Orion Business Books.
Corriere, Dr Richard and McGrady, Patrick. 1986. *Life zones*. Ballantine Books.
Covey, Stepen R. 1994. *The seven habits of highly effective people*. Simon & Schuster.

De Becker, Gavin. 1997. *The gift of fear*. Bloomsbury.
De Jager, Melodie. 2001. *Breingim*. Human & Rousseau.

Ferreira, Annelie. 1995. *Daar's 'n mens binne*. Queillerie.
Field, Lynda. 1993. *Ontwikkel jou selfbeeld*. Tafelberg.
Field, Lynda. 1997. *60 Tips for self-esteem*. Element Books.
Fourie, Dawie. 1998. *Ontgin jou brein*. J.L. van Schaik.
Freedman, Joshua M. et al. 1998. *The handle with care emotional intelligence activity book*. Six Seconds.

Goleman, Daniel. 1996. *Emotional intelligence*. Bloomsbury.
Goleman, Daniel. 1998. *Working with emotional intelligence*. Bloomsbury.
Gottman, John. 1999. *The seven principles for making marriage work*. Weidenfield & Nicolson.
Gottman, John. 1997. *Why marriages succeed or fail*. Bloomsbury.
Greenberger, Dennis and Padesky, Christine A. 1995. *Mind over mood*. Guilford Press.
Grové, Shani. 1997. *Dankie, brein*. Human & Rousseau.
Grové, Shani. 1996. *Die brein-boek vir vroue en sommige mans*. Queillerie.
Grové, Shani. 1994. *Die dans van die brein*. Human & Rousseau.

Hattingh, Brenda. 1996. *Verandering: verleentheid of geleentheid*. Perskor.
Hein, Steve. 1998. "Emotional literacy." Information from Internet. Website has been changed. His current website is at *http://eqi.org /index.htm*
Holden, R. 1998. *Happiness NOW! Timeless wisdom for feeling good FAST*. Hodder & Stoughton.
Holmes, Ros and Holmes, Jeremy. 1998. *The good mood guide*. Orion.

Johnson, David. 1981. *Reaching out. Interpersonal effectiveness and self-acualization*. Prentice-Hall.
Jude, Dr Brian L. 1997. *Body language the South African way*. Delta Books.

Kruger, N. 1998. *Facilitating life skills*. Amabuhu Publications.

Le Doux, Joseph. 1998. *The emotional brain*. Weidenfield & Nicolson.
Lindenfield, Gael. 1997. *Emotional confidence*. Thorsons.
Lindenfield, Gael. 1995. *Self-esteem*. Thorsons.
Lindenfield, Gael. 1989. *Super confidence*. Thorsons.
Lipkin, Mike. 1998. *Mampodi!!* Human & Rousseau.

Mangham, Colin. 1995. "Resiliency: Relevance to health promotion discussion paper." Atlantic Health Promotion Research Centre. Dalhousie University.
Mann, Sandi. 1999. *Hiding what you feel, faking what we don't*. Element Books.
Meyer, Jack; Salovey, Peter and Caruso, David. *Emotional IQ Test*. CD-Rom from LifestylesGold series.
McCown, Karen S. et al. 1998. *Self-science*. Six Seconds.
McKay Matthew et al. 1997. *Thoughts and feelings*. New Harbinger.
Miller, Tom. Video. *Self-discipline and emotional control*. Career Track Videos.
*Mindpower series*. Time-Life Books.
Morcher, Dr Betsy and Jones, Dr Barbara S. 1992. *Successful risk-taking for women. Go for it*. Warner Books.

National Council for Mental Health. 1990. *Lewensvaardighede vir self-ontwikkeling*.
Newman, Margaret. 1994. *Stepfamily realities*. New Harbinger.

Omartian, Stormie. 1999. *Emosionele vryheid*. Struik Christelike Boeke.

Perry, Mitchell. *In the zone. Achieving optimal performance in business/as in sports*. Video from Learning Technologies.
Pert, Candice B. 1997. *Molecules of emotion. Why you feel the way you feel*. Pocket Books.
Phillips, Maya. 1997. *Emotional excellence. A course in self-mastery*. Element Books.
Phillips, Maya. 1999. *Emotional excellence. A practical guide to self-discovery*. Element Books.
Plug et al. 1991. *Psigologiewoordeboek*. Lexicon.
Potter-Efron, Ronald T. 1998. *Working anger*. New Harbinger.

Ruskan, John. 1998. *Emotional clearing*. Random House.
Rutledge, Thom. 1997. *The self-forgiveness handbook*. New Harbinger.

Salovey, Peter and Sluyter, David J. 1997. *Emotional development and emotional intelligence. Educational implications*. Basic Books.
Schilling, Dianne. 1990. *50 activities for teaching emotional intelligence*. Innerchoice Publishing.
Segal, Jeanne. 1997. *Raising your emotional intelligence*. Henry Holt and Company.
Simmons, Steve and Simmons, John C. 1997. *Measuring emotional intelligence*. The Summit Publishing Group.
Somer, Elizabeth. 1999. *Food and mood*. Henry Holt Publishing.
Steiner, Claude and Perry Paul. 1997. *Achieving emotional literacy*. Bloomsbury.
Steiner, Claude and Perry, Paul. 1977. *Emotional literacy*. Clays Ltd.

Viscott, David. 1996. *Emotional resilience*. Three Rivers Press.

Weisinger, Hendrie. 1998. *Emotional intelligence at work*. Jossey-Bass Publishers.
Wilks, Francis. 1996. *Intelligent emotion*. William Heineman.

# ENDNOTES

1. Melodie de Jager can be contacted at Brain Dynamics in Johannesburg or at the following e-mail address: *melodiedj@worldonline.co.za*
2. Steiner, Claude, *Achieving emotional literacy*, 1997. Used with the permission of C. Steiner.
3. Pert, Candice, *Molecules of emotion*, 1997.
4. Goleman, Daniel, *Emotional intelligence*, 1995.
5. Simmons, Steve and Simmons, John D., *Measuring emotional intelligence*, 1997.
6. Segal, Jeanne, *Raising your emotional intelligence*, 1997.
7. *Emotional IQ Test*, CD-Rom from LifestylesGold Series.
8. Jensen, Anabel and Freedman, Joshua, "The assessment and development of EQ (Six Seconds)" – course attended in Johannesburg, October 1999.
9. Johnson, David, *Reaching out*, 1981.
10. Ferreira, Annelie, *Daar's 'n mens binne*, 1995.
11. Course done on brain profiling at Brain Dynamics, Johannesburg, 1998.
12. Fourie, Dawie, *Ontgin jou brein*, 1998.
13. Authors may be approached by e-mail for more information.
14. Miller, Tom, *Self-discipline and emotional control*. Video No 3, Career Track Videos.
15. Jensen, A. and Freedman, J., "The assessment and development of EQ (Six Seconds)" – course attended during October 1999.
16. Ask authors by e-mail.
17. National Council for Mental Health, *Lewensvaardighede vir self-ontwikkeling*, 1990.
18. National Council for Mental Health, *Lewensvaardighede vir self-ontwikkeling*, 1990.
19. Field, Lynda, *Ontwikkel jou selfbeeld*, 1993.
20. National Council for Mental Health, *Lewensvaardighede vir self-ontwikkeling*, 1990.
21. Weisinger, Hendrie, *Emotional intelligence at work*, 1998.
22. Hein, Steve, "Emotional literacy", 1998. Internet. Current website is at: *http://eqi.org/index.htm*
23. Hein, Steve, "Emotional literacy", 1998. Internet. Current website is at: *http://eqi.org/index.htm*
24. Miller, Tom, *Self-discipline and emotional control*. Video No 2, Career Track Videos.
25. Goleman, Daniel, *Emotional intelligence*, 1995.
26. Used with the permission of Melodie de Jager: *melodiedj@worldonline.co.za*
27. Somer, Elizabeth, *Food and mood*, 1999.
28. Carnegie, Dale, *Hoe om kommer te verdryf en te begin leef*, 1986.
29. Weisinger, Hendrie, *Emotional intelligence at work*, 1998.
30. Potter-Efron, Ronald, *Working anger*, 1998.
31. Mangham, Colin, "Resiliency: Relevance to health promotion discussion paper", 1995.
32. Weisinger, Hendrie, *Emotional intelligence at work*, 1998.
33. Perry, J.M., *In the zone. Achieving optimal performance in business/as in sports*. Video from Learning Technologies.
34. Covey, Stephen, *The seven habits of highly effective people*, 1994.
35. Weisinger, Hendrie, *Emotional intelligence at work*, 1998.